Don't Quit! Your Faith Will See You Through

Kenneth Hagin Jr.

D1531397

Unless otherwise indicated, all Scripture quotations in this volume are from the *King James Version* of the Bible.

Third Printing 1995

ISBN 0-89276-724-3

In the U.S. write:
Kenneth Hagin Ministries
P.O. Box 50126
Tulsa, OK 74150-0126

In Canada write:
Kenneth Hagin Ministries
P.O. Box 335, Station D,
Etobicoke (Toronto), Ontario
Canada, M9A 4X3

BOOKS BY KENNETH E. HAGIN

Following God's Plan For Your Life
The Triumphant Church: Dominion Over All the Powers of Darkness
Healing Scriptures
Mountain Moving Faith
Love: The Way to Victory
The Price Is Not Greater Than God's Grace (Mrs. Oretha Hagin)

MINIBOOKS (A partial listing)

* The New Birth
* Why Tongues?
* In Him
* God's Medicine
* You Can Have What You Say
* Don't Blame God
* Words
  Plead Your Case
* How To Keep Your Healing
  The Bible Way To Receive the Holy Spirit
  I Went to Hell
  How To Walk in Love
  The Precious Blood of Jesus
* Love Never Fails
  How God Taught Me About Prosperity

BOOKS BY KENNETH HAGIN JR.

* Man's Impossibility — God's Possibility
  Because of Jesus
  How To Make the Dream God Gave You Come True
  The Life of Obedience
  God's Irresistible Word
  Healing: Forever Settled
  Don't Quit! Your Faith Will See You Through
  The Untapped Power in Praise
  Listen to Your Heart
  What Comes After Faith?
  Speak to Your Mountain!
  Come Out of the Valley!
  It's Your Move!
  God's Victory Plan

MINIBOOKS (A partial listing)

* Faith Worketh by Love
* Seven Hindrances to Healing
* The Past Tense of God's Word
  Faith Takes Back What the Devil's Stolen
      How To Be a Success in Life
  Get Acquainted With God
      Unforgiveness
  Ministering to the Brokenhearted

*These titles are also available in Spanish. Information about other foreign translations of several of the above titles (i.e., Finnish, French, German, Indonesian, Polish, Russian, etc.) may be obtained by writing to: Kenneth Hagin Ministries, P.O. Box 50126, Tulsa, Oklahoma 74150-0126.

Contents

Preface

This book was written with a heart to help and to encourage God's people wherever they may be and in whatever situations they may find themselves in life. Let's face it, at some time or another, we are all confronted with challenging obstacles. But we must realize that it's not our own strength that will put us over in life. And one objective of this book is to look at the lives of some of the men and women of the Bible, many of whom were ordinary people just like you and me, and see the insurmountable obstacles they faced and how their faith in God brought them through to victory every time! These were people who had every opportunity to quit at times when everything seemed to be against them. These weren't necessarily great men and women, but they were men and women with *great* faith in a *great* God. By looking at their lives and the tests and trials they faced — we can learn valuable lessons from them for our own "fight of faith" in the day and hour in which we live. May God's people realize that holding on to God's Word in every trying circumstance and in every difficult situation — no matter how impossible it may look — is the only way to truly be successful in life. God will always make a way for us! And God's message to us is still the same today as it has always been: "Don't Quit! Keep trusting Me. Your faith in Me will see you through!"

Chapter 1
God's Timeless Message to You

Throughout the Bible, from the very first pages of Genesis to the last pages of the Book of Revelation, God gives His people the same loving, timeless message: "Don't give up! Keep on trusting Me! *I* will bring you through any difficulty and *I* will make you victorious in life!" God in His mercy has interwoven this message throughout the Word of God because He desires to encourage and inspire mankind, knowing His creation will face challenging obstacles in life from time to time. And because of the challenges and opposition we do sometimes face in life, there's probably not one person who has ever lived upon this earth who hasn't at one time or another thought, *What's the use! I might just as well give up!*

However, we must realize that sometimes even the great patriarchs of the Bible — from Abraham the father of many nations to the Apostle John who penned the Book of Revelation on the Isle of Patmos — were faced with many of the same questions, perplexities, and trials we've faced in our own generation. In the face of sometimes insurmountable difficulties, godly men and women in the Bible had to make the same decision Christians today must make: *Should I quit? Should I just give up and forget what God has promised me? Can I really believe that what God has promised, He is able also to perform?*

As we look into the Bible, we need to see some of these examples of God's people who faced opportunities to quit at times when everything seemed to be against them. And it would be an encouragement to our faith to look at the lives of some of them to see how their faith in God brought

1

them through the hard times and the tests and trials of life. In many cases, they were just ordinary people like you and me. They came from all walks of life and every stratum of society: Abraham the father of many nations; Daniel, Shadrach, Meshach, and Abednego — princes of Israel; Samson, a man separated, called, and chosen by God to do a mighty work in Israel; blind Bartimaeus — a poor hopeless wretch who lived by the side of the road begging alms of those more fortunate in life than he; the woman with the issue of blood — as far as we know just an ordinary woman of her day who dared to believe God; the man taken with palsy — a man who would not allow circumstances to daunt his faith — and his four friends who demonstrated their unity of faith; and the man at the Gate Beautiful, who refused to take his eyes off the goal.

We can see that these weren't necessarily *great* men and women, but they were men and women who had great *faith* in a great *God.* They had great faith because when confronted with impossibilities, they didn't just give up! They held on tenaciously to their faith in God! They knew what it was to struggle to believe God in the face of all contradictory and opposing circumstances. Therefore, although these men and women may not have been particularly *great* in themselves, what made them notable was their steadfast faith in a *great God.* Instead of quitting when confronted with challenges, they each made a far-reaching decision. That decision would ultimately extend into eternity for each of them and cause their triumph of faith to be recorded in the Word of God; that decision was *to press on and to trust God in the face of all contradictory and opposing circumstances!* Should we do any less?

Each of us, at some time in our lives, will be presented

with the same decision. God has given to each of us promises in His Word and many times He has revealed to us
aspects of His plan for our lives. But when everything
looks bleak all around us — when there seems to be no
possible hope for receiving what God has promised us —
shall we abandon all hope in what God has told us?

By looking at their lives and the challenges these men
and women of great faith faced and how their faith in God
overcame every trial, it will encourage our faith for the
challenges we must face, and the decisions we must make
in our own lives. We can be encouraged by their lives —
the victories, the pitfalls, the trying circumstances, and
even the struggles they endured to keep their faith in God
strong in the face of all opposing circumstances which
seemed to scream at them, "You can't make it! You're
going to fail! There's no way you can do what God has
told you to do!"

Also, by looking at the lives of men and women of great
faith who suffered with the same weaknesses of the flesh
as we do, and who struggled with their own human inade-
quacies and inabilities just as we do — we will see that
they didn't overcome the obstacles to their faith *in their
own strength*. Their *faith in God* was the secret of their
success. It was their faith in a *faithful* God that caused
them to be overcomers in life. They believed God would
bring them through every difficulty and through every
trial into what He had promised them. What a challenge
to our faith to believe God in spite of every opposition for
the fulfillment of His plan in our lives too!

Time after time we see in the Word that these godly
men and women of the Bible realized they could not get
the best God had for them if they quit believing and

trusting in God. Quitting would gain them *nothing,* but wholeheartedly following God would gain them *everything!* Each of them had to make the choice whether or not they would give up or whether they would keep on trusting God and walking in His ways even when every circumstance seemed to make the fulfillment of God's promise *impossible.* Quitting would have been the easy way out. It took faith to stand! In every circumstance, *it was perseverance of faith* that brought them through!

As an encouragement to our own faith, let's look at the faith and the lives of some of these men and women of the Bible and see how their faith in God brought them through the difficulties they faced. They did not live problem-free lives. And if *they* faced adverse circumstances — "the giants" of their day, yet they tenaciously believed God, and in His strength overcame every trial which came their way, then *we* can too. We can learn from them that faith in God will always see us through no matter what the difficulty, no matter what the trial, and no matter what the circumstance! No matter how high that mountain seems to be, with God's help, you *can* overcome it!

Abraham's Test of Faith

We know that Abraham is called, "The Father of Many Nations." We hear that and we're sometimes tempted to think, *Well, Abraham had it made! Everything he did turned out right because God especially favored him. He was never faced with the trials I'm faced with in life!*

Nothing could be further from the truth! Let's look at Abraham's life and see how his faith in God saw him through, and how he overcame the obstacles he faced.

Whether you realize it or not, there are *no* successful men or women of God in the Bible who at one time or another were not faced with insurmountable obstacles which *they could not overcome in themselves.*

If you'll study the Word, you'll see that God told every great man or woman of faith to do something which seemed absolutely impossible for him or her to do! God knew it was impossible for each of them to accomplish in their *own* strength what He had set before them because God is *the God of the impossible. He* wants to do the impossible *through* His people. God always has goals that are impossible for His people to achieve or accomplish in themselves, because His thoughts are above our thoughts, and His ways are above our ways (Isa. 55:8). But He sets these impossible goals for His people because He wants them to learn to totally rely *on Him* to accomplish His will in their lives. God knows that in ourselves we can do nothing, but that *through Him* nothing is impossible. With God all things are possible. And if we can ever get out of the way and let God perform the impossible that He's promised us, He'll do it!

Faith that dares to believe God to accomplish the impossible, pleases God! Besides that, allowing God to perform the impossible in our lives gives *God* all the glory!

You see, God's people can do *the ordinary,* but God knows we can't do *the impossible!* And God is looking for His people to rely on Him to do the impossible in their lives! Their faith in Him will see them through!

Let's see how God worked out the impossible in Abraham's life. For a long time Abraham had wanted a son but it was a *human* impossibility because Sarah and Abraham were both well past the age for having children.

Did that stop God from fulfilling His promise to give them a son? No! When it was impossible in the *natural,* God promised to *supernaturally* bring His promise to pass in their lives! But Abraham had to keep on believing in the God who had promised and in the God who is more than enough to fulfill His promises. Abraham had to believe that God was bigger than any problem or circumstance and that He was able to keep His Word. Abraham could have quit and given up when it looked as if God's promise of a son was not going to come to pass. But Abraham didn't give up! He refused to quit.

The secret to Abraham's strong faith was that he kept looking *to God* instead of looking *at his problem.* That should be a lesson to us! Finally, after all human hope was gone, God fulfilled His Word to Abraham and gave Abraham and Sarah a son — Isaac — the son of promise. Why did God wait so long to fulfill His promise to Abraham and Sarah? Because for one thing, when all *human* hope and ability were gone, then it was time for God to move *supernaturally.* By that time there was no earthly way Abraham and Sarah could bring God's promise of a child to pass. When man's resources are at an end, then God performs the miraculous and brings to pass *His* promise and His purposes. That way, God gets all the glory!

You may have a problem or a trial you've faced in your life which you've tried to overcome. Some of you may even have said, "I've fought this battle for so long, what's the use? I'll never win." But have you been fighting it in your own strength? Or have you put all your trust in God and in His Word? Because I want you to know that the Bible says, "*. . . The things which are IMPOSSIBLE with men* *are POSSIBLE with God"* (Luke 18:27). Just remember, God delights in man's *impossibilities.* Every impossible obstacle is an opportunity *and* a possibility with God — if you just won't quit. If you won't quit, your faith in God will see you through to the other side of that problem to victory!

Hold on to your faith in God, just as Abraham did. When Abraham's son, Isaac, finally came along, Abraham had great cause to rejoice in God's faithfulness to His promise. In this test of his faith, Abraham found out that Isaac was to be "the son of promise" not the son of *human* ability (*See* Genesis chapters 17 and 18). Abraham believed God even when human hope was gone; he knew that his faith in the God of the impossible would not go unrewarded.

You might think that once Abraham's long-awaited promise of a son was fulfilled, all his problems and trials would be over. But God has a way of testing the obedience of His children, and the time came when God tested Abraham's obedience. God required Abraham to offer up Isaac — the son for whom he'd waited so long — as a sacrifice to Him! You can imagine what an opportunity that was for Abraham to give up and lose faith in God. Abraham could have said, "What's the use! I quit! I waited for years to get a son, and now You're requiring me to put him on the altar and give him back to You!"

GENESIS 22:1-14
1   And it came to pass after these things, that God did tempt [prove or test] Abraham, and said unto him, Abraham: and he said, Behold, here I am.
2   And he said, Take now thy son, thine only son Isaac, whom thou lovest, and get thee into the land of Moriah;

and offer him there for a burnt offering upon one of the mountains which I will tell thee of.

3   And Abraham rose up early in the morning, and saddled his ass, and took two of his young men with him, and Isaac his son, and clave the wood for the burnt offering, and rose up, and went unto the place of which God had told him.

4   Then on the third day Abraham lifted up his eyes, and saw the place afar off.

5   And Abraham said unto his young men, Abide ye here with the ass; and I and the lad will go yonder and worship, and come again to you.

6   And Abraham took the wood of the burnt offering, and laid it upon Isaac his son; and he took the fire in his hand, and a knife; and they went both of them together.

7   And Isaac spake unto Abraham his father, and said, My father: and he said, Here am I, my son. And he said, Behold the fire and the wood: but where is the lamb for a burnt offering?

8   And Abraham said, My son, GOD WILL PROVIDE himself a lamb for the burnt offering: so they went both of them together.

9   And they came to the place which God had told him of; and Abraham built an altar there, and laid the wood in order, and bound Isaac his son, and laid him on the altar upon the wood.

10 And Abraham stretched forth his hand, and took the knife to slay his son.

11 And the angel of the Lord called unto him out of heaven, and said, Abraham, Abraham: and he said, Here am I.

12 And he said, Lay not thine hand upon the lad, neither do thou any thing unto him: for now I know that thou fearest God, seeing thou hast not withheld thy son, thine only son from me.

13 And Abraham lifted up his eyes, and looked, and behold behind him a ram caught in a thicket by his horns: and Abraham went and took the ram, and offered him up for a burnt offering in the stead of his son.

14 And Abraham called the name of that place Jehovah-jireh [God will see to it or GOD WILL PROVIDE]: as it is said to this day, In the mount of the Lord it shall be seen.

Abraham didn't waver or lose his trust and confidence in God even when God required a hard thing of him — to sacrifice his son. That *tested* his faith. But even after God had commanded Abraham to offer Isaac as a sacrifice, notice Abraham's faith-filled confession: "... *God will provide* ..." (Gen. 22:8).

That statement showed Abraham's commitment to God. Abraham was so committed to God that he acted in faith to carry out God's will without regard to what it would cost him *personally* — even to the sacrificing of his own son, Isaac. That's dedication to God!

Each one of us needs to ask ourselves, *Do I have that quality of dedication and faith in God?* God is not going to require you to *literally* offer a son or daughter upon an altar to Him. But He is going to test your commitment to Him. And it will take that same quality of determined faith and commitment to God that Abraham had in order for God to bring about what He has promised *you*.

Abraham was so dedicated to God and his faith in the promises of God was so firm and immovable, that he trusted God to provide for him no matter what the circumstances looked like. That's the key! He didn't look at the *circumstances;* he looked to *God!* And at the last minute, God provided a ram that was caught in a thicket to use as a sacrifice instead of Abraham's son, Isaac (Gen. 22:13).

You see, when the trials of life came, the patriarchs of the Bible had to make the choice — just as you and I do — whether or not they would believe God and continue to serve Him. At any point in their walk with God they could have said, "This is too hard! Forget it!" In the trials of life that came to them — just as in the trials of life which

come to you and me — God didn't *make* them do anything.
God didn't force them to keep on trusting Him, anymore
than He compels us to keep on trusting Him. Of course,
He desires our trust; He knows that He alone is trust-
worthy and that He alone can bring to pass His purposes
in our lives. But the overcomers of the Bible had to make
the choice to trust God completely, and so do we.

The Apostle John is another great patriarch of the
Bible who had every opportunity to quit and to give up.
John's faith was tested — John, the great apostle who
wrote the Book of Revelation!

We see in studying Church history that there were
those who tried to kill John in every way they could.
According to historical tradition, Roman authorities even
tried to boil John alive in oil, but they still couldn't kill
him. Unable to destroy this godly man of faith, they finally
exiled him to the Isle of Patmos. In every trial the enemy
brought against him, John refused to give up. He refused
to quit, and he refused to let go of his faith in God!

Throughout the Bible, God tells us not to quit! The
Holy Spirit exhorts and encourages us on every page of
God's Word that we are not to give up — our faith in God
will see us through every time! God's repeated message
to us in the Bible is that we are to keep on believing and
trusting in Him and He will cause us to be victorious over
any trial, *any* circumstance, and *any* difficulty!

Mark 9:23 says, "*. . . all things are possible to him that
believeth.*" That means *all* things! That means *anything*
is possible with God if you'll only believe and trust in Him!
If your desires line up with God's Word and His will for
your life, then with God on your side, *nothing* is impossible for you!

I have yet to see God fail to answer the sincere cry of someone with a heart of faith. I have yet to see an individual go under or fail when he or she sincerely began to believe God and take Him at His Word. But too many Christians are quitting and forsaking their faith in God and selling God short! Don't quit! That's just what Satan wants; he wants you to quit. Don't get discouraged! Your faith in God will see you through!

Walking by Faith or by Sight?

So many Christians — sincere, Bible-believing Christians — want *to live by faith,* but at the same time, they want *to walk by sight.* In what ways do they want to walk by sight? For one thing, many want to have the whole plan of God for their lives laid out in front of them before they will even take *one* step of faith or obedience. That's not walking by faith — that's walking by sight.

Also, when you walk by faith, you've got to make up your mind not to quit — I don't care if circumstances seem so dark, you can only see *one* step in front of you. Faith takes that *one* step!

As you take just one step at a time in faith, determine in your heart to live by the Word of God and to never quit or turn back. If you'll do that, sooner than you think, you'll look back and see just how far you've come! That's how you will walk *by faith* over any mountain or across any valley, through any trouble or around any adverse circumstance. One step of faith and obedience can bring you into the joy of the Lord and the fulfillment of the promise of God in your life.

On the other hand, if you try to figure out everything

God has for you before you begin taking those steps of faith, and you try to see further down the road than what God is ready to reveal to you, you'll get yourself in a mess and maybe drag others along with you too.

Success the Bible Way

Of course you want to be a success in life; everyone does. But how many of you are really making the *commitment* to be the success God wants you to be? It's true that you will have many opportunities to quit in life, but you'll have just as many opportunities to succeed! Instead of worrying about failing, use every opportunity to put your trust in God for success! Yes, the devil will try to bring circumstances against you which will test you. But it's during those times when you will find out whether or not you really believe what you say you believe!

Oh, it's easy to make confessions of faith as long as you're in church or surrounded by your Christian friends. It's easy to tell your friends what you're believing God for and to brag about what God is going to do for you. But what about when you are out there in the tests and trials of life all by yourself? What about those times when there's no one else with you — no friends or anyone to help you or to pray with you!

I guarantee you, there will be those times when you will be alone, just you and God, and you will have to depend totally on Him and on His Word. There may even come the time when you'll find yourself all alone in a situation, and you might wonder why. But God will put you in situations that will cause you to grow. God wants you to grow! That's when you'll find out if your faith in God's

Word is real, or if you are just "trying out this faith business."

It's during the hard times when you find out what your faith is made of! Do you really believe God will do what He said He would do? In the hard times — in the times of tests and trials — it will be your faith and commitment to God and your determination to believe His Word that will carry you through. Without that faith *and* commitment to God you will probably be defeated. That's not a negative statement. But there will be those times in life which come to us all when it seems that Satan uses every opportunity to try to stop the plan of God in our lives and tries to render us ineffective in life and in ministry.

But just remember: It's not the *opportunity* to fail that makes you fail in life, because opportunities to fail and quit come to us all. It's what you *do* with those opportunities that determine whether or not you will fail. Will you choose to go to God and stand upon His Word regardless of the trial or circumstance? Or will you just throw up your hands and say, "That's it! I quit! God's Word doesn't work!"?

When you look at it like this, you can see that it's up to each one of us whether or not we succeed or fail in life. Those who persevere in God *will* succeed. You see, *God* doesn't make failures. *People* make failures when they stop short of their success in God! The sad thing is many people quit just short of reaching the success in God they've been desiring all along.

Let's look in the Word of God at a well-known man of faith who turned every difficulty into an opportunity to trust God. This godly man had such a strong commitment and determination to follow God that he succeeded in every area of life. Daniel was that man. Daniel was whole-heartedly committed to God. No, he didn't always have it easy in life, but his faith in God was firm and immovable — and his faith saw him through every difficulty he faced!

Chapter 2
Success Means
Strong Commitment to God

The great and thriving city of Jerusalem which was nestled so beautifully in the Judean countryside, was ravaged by the Babylonians in the sixth century B.C. Certain Jews from the royal house of Israel were carried off into captivity to Babylon. Babylon was at that time one of the greatest empires in history.

The Babylonian Empire had conquered all of the then-known world. And it was a Babylonian practice to take the elite of a conquered nation — the nobles, rulers, and leaders — back to Babylon to be used in key positions in government and leadership, or to assist in other areas where the captives were particularly gifted or useful. In this way, Babylon not only possessed a conquered and dispossessed nation, but the Babylonians also had at their disposal a great work force comprised of "the cream of the crop" of trained and gifted Hebrews — really, a work force of slaves.

Among those taken in captivity to Babylon were four young Hebrew princes: Daniel (renamed Belteshazzar), Hananiah (Shadrach), Mishael (Meshach), and Azariah (Abednego). The Bible tells us that these Hebrews had favor with King Nebuchadnezzar, the ruling Babylonian king at that time (Dan. 1:17-20).

Let's look first at Daniel's life and see the overwhelmingly opposing circumstances that confronted him, and discover what he did to overcome them.

First, we need to realize that when Daniel was taken to live in captivity in Babylon, he had every opportunity to do as the Babylonians did — to live as they did, to worship their false gods, and to follow in the ways of their corrupt religious practices. As a Hebrew captive in a foreign country, perhaps no one would have known it. There was certainly no one to enforce Daniel's strict Hebraic upbringing upon him and to demand that he remain steadfast to God.

But Daniel made a decision and that decision was the secret to his success in life. In fact, it is interesting to note that Daniel's success can be traced back to the godly decisions he made *when he was in the hard place* in life — when the tests and trials tried to overwhelm him, exiled as he was in far-off Babylon! It was in Babylon, in what some would call the "valley," where we see Daniel's immovable and unshakable devotion to God, even though his faith was under extreme testing. And the decisions Daniel made — just as the decisions you and I make — were crucial because they helped determine the course his life would take.

We'll see that it was while he was exiled in Babylon — when he was in *the hard place* — that Daniel made a crucial decision which set the stage for his future success: He *purposed in his heart not to defile himself* by compromising his faith in God (Dan 1:8). He determined to do only those things which were pleasing and right in the sight of God. He vowed in his heart to remain steadfast to God — no matter what the consequences!

And we'll see that because Daniel purposed in his heart to be pleasing to God, even though he had to walk through some fiery trials, in the end God promoted him so that he became one of the most important men in the entire Babylonian Empire.

Daniel was a Hebrew, probably of royal descent (Dan. 1:3). According to Jewish Law, eating the king's meat would defile Daniel, because it would violate his Hebraic training and his godly upbringing. We must remember that Daniel was under the Old Covenant and therefore subject to Jewish Law. Daniel wanted only to please God, and, for Daniel, to displease God meant *failure*. God is a rewarder of those who desire to please him!

DANIEL 1:3-8

3   And the king [Nebuchadnezzar] spake unto Ashpenaz the master of his eunuchs, that he should bring certain of the children of Israel, and of the king's seed, and of the princes;

4   Children in whom was no blemish, but well favoured, and skilful in all wisdom, and cunning in knowledge, and understanding science, and such as had ability in them to stand in the king's palace, and whom they might teach the learning and the tongue of the Chaldeans.

5   And the king appointed them a daily provision of the king's meat, and of the wine which he drank: so nourishing them three years, that at the end thereof they might stand before the king.

6   Now among these were the children of Judah, Daniel, Hananiah, Mishael, and Azariah:

7   Unto whom the prince of the eunuchs gave names: for he gave unto Daniel the name of Belteshazzar; and to Hananiah, of Shadrach; and to Mishael, of Meshach; and to Azariah, of Abednego.

8   BUT DANIEL PURPOSED IN HIS HEART that HE WOULD NOT DEFILE HIMSELF with the portion of the king's meat, nor with the wine which he drank: therefore he requested of the prince of the eunuchs that he might not defile himself.

As you read the continuation of Daniel chapter 1, you

will see some of the results of Daniel's resolve not to defile himself, but to be pleasing to God instead.

> **DANIEL 1:17,19-20**
> **17 As for these four children [Daniel, Shadrach, Meshach, and Abednego], God gave them knowledge and skill in all learning and wisdom: and Daniel had understanding in all visions and dreams....**
> **19 And the king communed with them; and among them all was found none like Daniel, Hananiah, Mishael, and Azariah: therefore stood they before the king.**
> **20 And in all matters of wisdom and understanding, that the king inquired of them, he found them ten times better than all the magicians and astrologers that were in all his realm.**

However, as we'll see, the circumstances got rough again when Daniel came up against laws and pressures imposed by a heathen king which were contrary to Daniel's commitment to God. Daniel's faith and resolve were again tested because a proclamation went forth that no one was to seek counsel of any man — or God — for thirty days. If anyone did, it meant death to that person! The person who defied the king's command would be thrown alive into a den of hungry lions!

How many of us have faced a lions' den because of our faith in God! That would be a test of faith, wouldn't it? Let's examine Daniel's faith in the midst of a circumstance which would probably daunt the faith of even the most courageous!

> **DANIEL 6:4-28**
> **4 Then the presidents and princes sought to find occasion against Daniel concerning the kingdom; but they could**

find none occasion nor fault; forasmuch as he was faithful, neither was there any error or fault found in him.

5   Then said these men, We shall not find any occasion against this Daniel, except we find it against him concerning the law of his God.

6   Then these presidents and princes assembled together to the king, and said. . . .

7   All the presidents of the kingdom, the governors, and the princes, the counsellors, and the captains, have consulted together to establish a royal statute, and to make a firm decree, that whosoever shall ask a petition of any God or man for thirty days, save of thee, O king, he shall be cast into the den of lions.

8   Now, O king, establish the decree, and sign the writing, that it be not changed, according to the law of the Medes and Persians, which altereth not.

9   Wherefore king Darius signed the writing and the decree.

10 Now WHEN DANIEL KNEW THAT THE WRITING WAS SIGNED, he went into his house; and his windows being open in his chamber toward Jerusalem, he kneeled upon his knees three times a day, and prayed, and gave thanks before his God as he did aforetime.

11 Then these men assembled, and found Daniel praying and making supplication before his God.

12 Then they came near, and spake before the king concerning the king's decree; Hast thou not signed a decree, that every man that shall ask a petition of any God or man within thirty days, save of thee, O king, shall be cast into the den of lions? The king answered and said, The thing is true, according to the law of the Medes and Persians, which altereth not.

13 Then answered they and said before the king, That Daniel, which is of the children of the captivity of Judah, regardeth not thee, O king, nor the decree that thou hast signed, but maketh his petition three times a day.

14 Then the king, when he heard these words, was sore displeased with himself, and set his heart on Daniel to deliver him: and he laboured till the going down of the sun

to deliver him.

15 Then these men assembled unto the king, and said unto the king, Know, O king, that the law of the Medes and Persians is, That no decree nor statute which the king establisheth may be changed.

16 Then the king commanded, and they brought Daniel, and cast him into the den of lions. Now the king spake and said unto Daniel, Thy god whom thou servest continually, he will deliver thee.

17 And a stone was brought, and laid upon the mouth of the den; and the king sealed it with his own signet, and with the signet of his lords; that the purpose might not be changed concerning Daniel.

18 Then the king went to his palace, and passed the night fasting: neither were instruments of musick brought before him: and his sleep went from him.

19 Then the king arose very early in the morning, and went in haste unto the den of lions.

20 And when he came to the den, he cried with a lamentable voice unto Daniel: and the king spake and said to Daniel, O Daniel, servant of the living God, is thy God, whom thou servest continually, able to deliver thee from the lions?

21 Then said Daniel unto the king, O king, live for ever.

22 My God hath sent his angel, and hath shut the lions' mouths, that they have not hurt me: forasmuch as BEFORE HIM INNOCENCY was found in me; and ALSO BEFORE THEE, O king, have I done no hurt.

23 Then was the king exceeding glad for him, and commanded that they should take Daniel up out of the den. So Daniel was taken up out of the den, and no manner of hurt was found upon him, because he believed in his God.

24 And the king commanded, and they brought those men which had accused Daniel, and they cast them into the den of lions, them, their children, and their wives; and the lions had the mastery of them, and brake all their bones in pieces or ever they came at the bottom of the den.

25 Then king Darius wrote unto ALL PEOPLE, NATIONS, and LANGUAGES, THAT DWELL IN ALL

THE EARTH; Peace be multiplied unto you.

26 I make a decree, That in every dominion of my kingdom men tremble and fear before the God of Daniel: for he is the living God, and stedfast for ever, and his kingdom that which shall not be destroyed, and his dominion shall be even unto the end.

27 He delivereth and rescueth, and he worketh signs and wonders in heaven and in earth, who hath delivered Daniel from the power of the lions.

28 So this Daniel prospered in the reign of Darius, and in the reign of Cyrus the Persian.

In verse 10 we see that Daniel's faith in God was fixed and his commitment to God was immovable. Instead of obeying a decree that would cause him to turn from God, he worshipped and praised God three times a day just as he had always done. Daniel could do this because his eyes and his faith were upon God alone; therefore, he knew God was able to deliver him.

Even though Daniel remained faithful to God, he still had to face the lions' den. That's important for us to see, because sometimes we think that when we walk with God there will be no tests or trials in life. We may not have to face a lions' den in our lives, but there will be trials that will test our faith! But don't quit; your faith in God will see you through!

Daniel's faith did not waver as he faced the lions' den. And his faith in God did not go unrewarded because God sent an angel to shut the mouths of those hungry lions. But the key to Daniel's success and triumph over the evil plan of the enemy is found in verse 22: *"My God hath sent his angel, and hath shut the lions' mouths, that they have not hurt me: forasmuch as before him INNOCENCY was*

*found in me; and also BEFORE THEE, O king, HAVE
I DONE NO HURT."*

In other words, Daniel was innocent before God *and*
man. So although evil men rose up against Daniel and tried
to destroy him, God protected him because Daniel walked
uprightly before God *and* man. Daniel was found blameless
in his ways before God; therefore, no evil scheme could
prosper against him! Not only that, but because Daniel's
ways pleased God, even though Daniel had to face this
trial, God promoted him so that he became one of the most
important men in the entire Babylonian Empire.

What's important for us to see in this passage of Scripture is that regardless of circumstances, because Daniel
purposed in his heart to please God, he put himself *in a
position* to receive from God.

If you keep your heart right before God *and* man, God
will take up your case, too, and you will always come out
a victor!

Chapter 3
Facing the Fire!

There were three other young Hebrew princes who had also been taken captive along with Daniel whose names were Shadrach, Meshach, and Abednego. They, too, came under extreme pressures to abandon their faith in God and to bow down to heathen gods and to false images.

In Daniel chapter 3, we see that just as Daniel's faith was tested, the faith of these three Hebrew princes was also sorely tested. King Nebuchadnezzar made an image of gold. He called together all the princes, rulers, and citizens of his kingdom and commanded that when music was played, everyone was to fall down and worship the king's golden image (Dan. 3:1-5). However, Shadrach, Meshach, and Abednego had purposed in their hearts to only serve and obey the one true God.

DANIEL 3:1,3-18

1 Nebuchadnezzar the king made an image of gold. . . .: he set it up in the plain of Dura, in the province of Babylon. . . .

3 Then [all the people] . . . were gathered together unto the dedication of the image that Nebuchadnezzar the king had set up; and they stood before the image that Nebuchadnezzar had set up.

4 Then an herald cried aloud, To you it is commanded, O people, nations, and languages,

5 That at what time ye hear the sound of . . . musick, ye fall down and worship the golden image that Nebuchadnezzar the king hath set up:

6 And whoso falleth not down and worshippeth shall the same hour be cast into the midst of a BURNING FIERY FURNACE.

7 Therefore at that time, when all the people heard the

sound of the ... musick, all the people, the nations, and the languages, fell down and worshipped the golden image that Nebuchadnezzar the king had set up.
8 Wherefore at that time certain Chaldeans came near, and accused the Jews.
9 They spake and said to the king Nebuchadnezzar, O king, live for ever.
10 Thou, O king, hast made a decree, that every man that shall hear the sound of ... musick, shall fall down and worship the golden image:
11 And whoso falleth not down and worshippeth, that he should be cast into the midst of a burning fiery furnace.
12 There are certain Jews whom thou hast set over the affairs of the province of Babylon, Shadrach, Meshach, and Abednego; these men, O king, have not regarded thee: they serve not thy gods, nor worship the golden image which thou hast set up.
13 Then Nebuchadnezzar in his rage and fury commanded to bring Shadrach, Meshach, and Abednego. Then they brought these men before the king.
14 Nebuchadnezzar spake and said unto them, Is it true, O Shadrach, Meshach, and Abednego, do not ye serve my gods, nor worship the golden image which I have set up?
15 Now if ye be ready that at what time ye hear the sound of the ... musick, ye fall down and worship the image which I have made; well: but if ye worship not, ye shall be cast the same hour into the midst of a burning fiery furnace; and who is that God that shall deliver you out of my hands?
16 Shadrach, Meshach, and Abednego, answered and said to the king, O Nebuchadnezzar, we are not careful to answer thee in this matter.
17 IF IT BE SO, our God whom we serve is able to deliver us from the burning fiery furnace, and he will deliver us out of thine hand, O king.
18 But if not, BE IT KNOWN UNTO THEE, O king, that WE WILL NOT SERVE THY GODS, nor worship the golden image which thou hast set up.

All the people of the kingdom were assembled together and when the music played, everyone bowed down to the golden image — that is, everyone except for the three young men who stood straight and tall for their God: Shadrach, Meshach, and Abednego.

When everyone else compromised and crumbled under the pressure to worship the king's golden image, you can imagine what strong faith and determination it took to remain standing tall and strong for God! Not to bow in worship of a false idol was an obvious and determined act of defiance against an ungodly decree. Think of the boldness that took! In the midst of that host of people who were prostrate before the king's idol, three strong young men standing boldly for their God was a rather obvious sight!

Shadrach, Meshach, and Abednego knew the consequences they would face by not bowing to the king's command — they knew it meant death to disobey the king's decree. But from childhood these Hebrews had been taught the Ten Commandments, and they knew better than to worship any other god except the God of Abraham, Isaac, and Jacob — the God of heaven and earth. But, after all, they were in a foreign nation — they weren't even in their own country. Maybe no one would have noticed if they had bowed down *just once* to escape that fiery furnace!

But strong faith doesn't turn back! Strong faith doesn't compromise, and strong faith doesn't quit under pressure! Strong faith tenaciously holds on to what *God* has said!

Shadrach, Meshach, and Abednego refused to quit or to compromise the call of God on their lives just to go along with the crowd. They refused to bow. In the face of probably the biggest test of their lives, they made a decision to stand for God — even if it meant death. There are rewards for a commitment like that! We will see how God promoted and honored them because of their strong stand for Him.

But first, notice two important truths in verses 17 and 18.

> DANIEL 3:17,18
> 17 If it be so, our GOD whom we serve IS ABLE TO DELIVER US from the burning fiery furnace, and he will deliver us out of thine hand, O king.
> 18 BUT IF NOT, be it known unto thee, O king, that WE WILL NOT SERVE THY GODS, nor worship the golden image which thou hast set up.

Some people have said that these two verses show a compromise of faith in these three Hebrews, and indicate that they were double-minded. These people say this because in verse 17, Shadrach, Meshach, and Abednego made a strong statement of faith in God: *"If it be so, our God whom we serve is able to deliver us. . . ."* But then in verse 18 the Hebrews seem to reverse their position of faith and compromise it by saying, *"BUT IF NOT* [In other words, if God doesn't deliver us]. . . *we will not serve thy gods. . . ."*

While it's true the Hebrews did say, "If God doesn't deliver us, we still won't serve your gods," we need to look at these verses in a little different light. We will discover that this was not a compromise of their faith at all! In fact, exactly the opposite is true! Let's examine these verses in the light of understanding *strong faith.*

You will never have *strong faith* without having accompanying *strong commitment.*

Verse 17 is a statement of the Hebrews' *faith* in a faithful God: "Our God is able to deliver us." It is a tremendous account of their trust in God's power. They *said* what they *believed;* that's *faith.*

Then they took a stand for their God; that's *commitment.* Verse 18 shows their *commitment* to God regardless of the circumstances that faced them. They said, "But if He doesn't, we will not serve your gods *no matter what.*" Their statement of commitment gave their faith *substance.* That commitment to their strong faith is what ultimately brought them favor and promotion from God: "No matter what happens, O king, we will not bow down and worship your false image!"

But as we will see, the faith of Shadrach, Meshach, and Abednego was tested in spite of their strong faith and persevering commitment. King Nebuchadnezzar had a furnace heated seven times hotter than usual, and when Shadrach, Meshach, and Abednego refused to compromise their faith in God, *they were thrown into it!* You think that wasn't an opportunity for their faith to falter!

DANIEL 3:19-30
19 Then was Nebuchadnezzar full of fury, and the form of his visage was changed against Shadrach, Meshach, and Abednego: therefore he spake, and commanded that they should heat the furnace one seven times more than it was wont to be heated.
20 And he commanded the most mighty men that were in his army to bind Shadrach, Meshach, and Abednego, and to cast them into the burning fiery furnace.
21 Then these men were bound in their coats, their hosen, and their hats, and their other garments, and were cast into the midst of the burning fiery furnace.
22 Therefore because the king's commandment was urgent,

and the furnace exceeding hot, the flame of the fire slew
those men that took up Shadrach, Meshach, and Abednego.
23 And these three men, Shadrach, Meshach, and Abednego, fell down bound into the midst of the burning fiery
furnace.
24 Then Nebuchadnezzar the king was astonied, and rose
up in haste, and spake, and said unto his counsellors, Did
not we cast three men bound into the midst of the fire?
They answered and said unto the king, True, O king.
25 He answered and said, Lo, I see four men loose, walking in the midst of the fire, and they have no hurt; and the
form of the fourth is like the Son of God.
26 Then Nebuchadnezzar came near to the mouth of the
burning fiery furnace, and spake, and said, Shadrach,
Meshach, and Abednego, ye servants of the most high God,
come forth, and come hither. Then Shadrach, Meshach, and
Abednego, CAME FORTH OF THE MIDST OF THE
FIRE.
27 And the princes, governors, and captains, and the king's
counsellors, being gathered together, saw these men, upon
whose bodies THE FIRE HAD NO POWER, nor was an
hair of their head singed, neither were their coats changed,
NOR THE SMELL OF FIRE HAD PASSED ON THEM.
28 Then Nebuchadnezzar spake, and said, Blessed be the
God of Shadrach, Meshach, and Abednego, who hath sent
his angel, and delivered his servants THAT TRUSTED IN
HIM, and HAVE CHANGED THE KING'S WORD, and
yielded their bodies, that they might not serve nor worship
any god, except their own God.
29 Therefore I make a decree, That every people, nation,
and language, which speak any thing amiss against the God
of Shadrach, Meshach, and Abednego, shall be cut in pieces,
and their houses shall be made a dunghill: because THERE
IS NO OTHER GOD THAT CAN DELIVER AFTER
THIS SORT.
30 Then the king PROMOTED Shadrach, Meshach, and
Abednego, in the province of Babylon.

Obedience to God wins favor with man. Notice how

Nebuchadnezzar's attitude changed toward Shadrach, Meshach, and Abednego all of a sudden. When he saw the mighty act of God, he began calling Shadrach, Meshach, and Abednego "servants of the most high God" (v. 26)! If you obey God, you'll win favor with man!

You talk about God getting the glory from the situation — look at verse 29: "... *there is no other God that can deliver after this sort.*" Because Shadrach, Meshach, and Abednego refused to quit and give up, not only did God deliver them, but they were promoted! That's what happens when you learn to live by faith and you are totally sold out in your commitment to God.

Now here's the point I want to get across. The faith of these three Hebrews was strong; they dared to believe God in spite of all opposition, *but their faith in God was still tested!*

It's not that we won't have tests and trials as Christians. But God will walk through every trial with us! And strong faith does not fail in a test or trial! The three Hebrew children had to walk through this fiery trial, all the while believing God for the victory. But in the final outcome, God not only rescued them out of their fiery ordeal, but He also promoted them for their faith in Him!

Your faith will be tested too! You may even go through a fiery trial or a fiery ordeal when you refuse to act like the world and when you take a strong stand of faith in God's Word. But your success is ultimately determined by your commitment to God and to His Word.

Another outcome of obedience and faith is that God gets glory. Because God delivered the three Hebrew children from the fiery furnace unharmed, King Nebuchadnezzar made a decree saying, "No one shall speak against the true God"

(v. 29). Also, because these three Hebrew princes dared
to believe God, King Nebuchadnezzar had to humble himself and admit, "The God of Shadrach, Meshach, and
Abednego made my word null and void!" (v. 28).

We need to see the magnitude of this event in the light
of Babylonian history. First, the Babylonian Empire had
swept across the known world at that time, conquering
nations which had previously been invincible. They were
the superpower of the world, and their rulers backed down
to no one, especially to those who served an unknown
foreign Hebrew God!

Second, once the king made a decree, it could not be
reversed (Dan. 6:8). Yet because of the courage of these
Hebrew princes who dared to have faith in God, this powerful king reversed his decree by saying, "I don't care who
made the decree! These Hebrews can serve their God
because when they refused to buckle under pressure, their
God had the power to deliver them!"

Also, I want you to notice that although the three
Hebrew princes, Shadrach, Meshach, and Abednego didn't
escape the fiery furnace, they did go through it unharmed.
They refused to turn back when the enemy and all the
cohorts of hell tried to discourage them from trusting God!
And because they stood for God in the face of death, not
even a trace of the *smell of smoke* from that fiery furnace
was evident on their clothes!

You know yourself that anytime you're close to a fire,
it's almost impossible to keep the smell of smoke out of
your clothes. So you can appreciate what a miracle this
was because Shadrach, Meshach, and Abednego were right
in the *midst* of that fire, yet there was no trace of smoke
on their clothing! They went through a fiery trial of their

faith, but God brought them safely through it unharmed.

You can have this same kind of victory in your life too. God promises His children in His Word that when you walk through a fiery trial, not even the smell of smoke will be upon your clothes! "... *when thou walkest through the fire, thou shalt not be burned; neither shall the flame kindle upon thee*" (Isa. 43:2).

This is the kind of faith you must develop in God if you want to be successful and achieve great victories in your life to God's glory. You don't need to worry about the future and what you may face in life; the God of great victories will see you through and the Word promises that as long as you stay in Christ, you'll be a victor!

Actually, this account in the Book of Daniel could have been penned this very day we live in. We may not be facing an actual fiery *furnace,* but we do face the tactics and the fiery trials of a deadly enemy, Satan. He not only has fiery trials, but he also has diseases, circumstances, and roadblocks of every kind that he tries to throw at us in life. But if we refuse to quit, *we cannot be defeated,* because God will deliver us from every fiery ordeal Satan may try to bring our way. And when God brings us out of a trial, the smell of smoke won't even be on our clothes! Just as God did with Shadrach, Meshach, and Abednego, if we'll keep our attitude right and keep our commitment to God steadfast, God will not only deliver us, but He'll see to it that we get promoted too!

You see, getting God's Word to work on your behalf is not a problem. The problem comes when God's people won't trust His Word! God is constantly trying to get His people to a position where they can receive all that He has for them.

But we can see by the lives of Shadrach, Meshach, and

Abednego, that to receive what God has for us in life depends on our faith and commitment to God and His Word.

And we can also see that our faith will need the backbone of strong commitment. Faith always makes a statement of commitment — an unwavering, uncompromising statement of what it is committed to do. Strong faith is always accompanied by strong commitment. If you are going to be a success in life and not quit, you must have *both* faith *and* commitment operating in your life.

You show me strong faith, and I'll show you strong commitment. The two go together! You cannot have strong faith without having strong commitment to God and His Word.

Faith with the commitment to back it up will see you through the hard times in life so you can reach the victory you so desire in God. If you think you can have strong faith without the backbone of strong commitment, you're just kidding yourself.

If you're not committed to what God has told you to do, then when you hit the tests and the trials in life — you'll turn and run. If you're not committed to God — to His *Word*, to His *plan* for your life, and to His *call* on your life — you'll have trouble maintaining your faith, especially in the hard times. But if you have really placed your life and your future in God's hands — you will be able to stand strong in faith no matter what test or trial comes along! Your faith in God won't fail when you have that kind of commitment!

There were many years when I was growing up that my father, Kenneth E. Hagin, was out in the field ministry preaching God's Word and teaching that God desires to prosper His people. My dad preached prosperity even when it seemed foolish to do so because we didn't have much money. But I can remember hearing the ring of commitment in his voice — even in trying times of financial lack. More than once I heard him say, "No matter what happens or what comes, sink or swim, live or die, we are going to live for God!" That's real commitment, and God can bless an individual who takes that kind of a stand for Him!

Some Christians are trying to walk by faith, but they have no commitment, so when the slightest trial comes up, they say, "Well, we'll *try* this faith business, but if it doesn't work, we can always *try* something else." You might just as well go try something else; faith won't work if you just *try* it because God knows, you know, and the devil knows that you're not committed to God and His Word!

HEBREWS 11:6
6   But without faith it is impossible to please him: for he that cometh to God must believe that he is, and that he is a rewarder of them that diligently seek him.

You see, the Bible says it's our *faith* that pleases God. But how can your faith please God if you're always wanting to give up in the trials of life! There's no backbone to that kind of faith!

This isn't to imply that Christians will always have trials and tribulations in life, because the Bible also talks about Christians enjoying life abundantly and that the joy of the Lord is our strength (John 10:10; Neh. 8:10). And the Bible says in Hebrews chapter 4 that there is a rest to the people of God, and that "... *we which have believed do enter into rest . . .''* (v. 3). But we must also realize that because Satan is the god of this world (2 Cor. 4:4), there will be tests and trials in life.

Strong faith and strong commitment are "buddies." To use an illustration — you can't shake hands with someone unless you have someone else's hand to shake. But if two people shake hands in agreement about something, they come into one accord on that issue. In the same way, when strong faith on the one hand comes into agreement with strong commitment on the other hand — that creates the kind of faith that will get something done on the earth to God's glory! That creates the same kind of explosive force for God as the natural and the supernatural coming together — it makes an explosive force for God!

You won't be defeated if you just won't quit! Shadrach, Meshach, and Abednego's strong faith was backed up by their strong commitment, so they not only succeeded but were *promoted.*

God can promote someone He can trust to stay faithful and to believe in Him. It will be the same way with you: God can deliver you out of any circumstance you're in if you are committed one hundred percent to Him and to His Word. But you must be completely sold out to Him!

Committed To Live Godly Lives

There is something else we need to see about commitment. You'll never be in a position to receive what God has for you if you have no commitment to live a godly life. Many Christians make the mistake of thinking, *Well, I can do what I want to do; no one will see me.* They act just like the crowd they're with at the time. If they associate with "faith" people, they talk "faith" talk. If they're with a worldly crowd, they begin to talk just like them. In other words, they don't really have any commitment to godly values themselves.

If Christians aren't committed to God's standards, they will act just like the world does. That's why many Christians have trouble living for God — they just aren't sold out to God. They think they can get by with compromise in their lives and still receive God's best! So they compromise their lifestyles and their values and then they wonder why their faith won't work and why they're missing out on God's blessings! God can't reward Christians who live like the world does.

If you are really committed to God, you'll always try to act in ways that please God, and it won't make any difference where you're at or who you're with; your integrity won't waver. The rewards for strong faith and strong commitment are not only *bountiful* but they are *eternal.* However, usually before the reward comes, your faith will be tested.

There is something else I want us to see in the lives of these three Hebrews. The decision whether these young Hebrew princes succeeded or failed did not rest with God, it was up to *them. They* chose what they would do that day when the music played and that great host of people were commanded to bow down to a graven image. Shadrach, Meshach, and Abednego had the choice of falling on their faces before that image and compromising their integrity with God, or they could choose to stand tall and firm in their commitment to God even though that meant facing a blazing fire. They decided to stand for God, so God stood for them!

If *you* stand for God, God will stand for *you* too!

You see, the decision to win — the decision to receive God's best — belongs to you, not to anyone else. No one else can make that decision for you. God has already provided everything for you in the redemption Christ purchased for you at the Cross. In His Word, God has already done everything He's ever going to do to ensure your full inheritance in Christ; it's available to you. Therefore, the decision whether you receive victory in every circumstance of life does not depend on God; it depends on *you*. It's your decision whether you just sit down and quit and let the devil have a heyday in your life, or whether you stand your ground and declare, "Oh, no you don't, Mr. Devil!"

Also, just as Daniel and the three Hebrew children made the commitment not to defile themselves, you're going to have to make that same decision. Make the commitment to fulfill God's will for your life — no matter what!

You may be facing fiery trials and obstacles in your life which you think are insurmountable, but I want to encourage you that with God's Word, you *can* succeed. Many people quit just at the point of success because so many circumstances have come against them in life. They feel as if life's problems have come against them on the right hand and on the left hand. They have come up against many obstacles and fought many battles, and they feel as if they have been stomped on by the enemy. After a while they begin to take the beaten-down attitude, *I might just as well throw in the towel. It's all over!*

But the man or the woman who understands faith and knows how to live by faith won't give up! When you are walking by faith, the enemy can fire every fiery dart at you and hurl every circumstance and problem he wants until your faith shield is so loaded down with his fiery darts that you feel as if you are staggering under the weight of it. The enemy can even fire what *appears* to be that *final shot* — just when you feel as if you are going to falter, stumble, and fall. You may be standing there reeling and rocking, but if you understand faith, you will just keep on saying more determined than ever, "I won't quit! I believe God!"

Others beside you who are weaker in faith may cry out, "I can't take it anymore! I give up!" But *you* will boldly confess, "I refuse to give up my faith in God and what He has promised me! The Word of God says I'm more than a conqueror in Christ Jesus. The Word says that greater is He that is in me than he that is in the world. I refuse to quit! I refuse to give up!"

About that time, you'll realize that the enemy has backed off from you when he hears you affirming your faith in God's Word. You'll notice that he's out of ammunition because he saw your faith could not be shaken since it's based on the Word of God. Then you'll shake yourself free from his every encumbrance, take that shield of faith, and begin walking toward the devil's onslaughts instead of running timidly away from them. You'll boldly declare God's Word and dismantle every weapon that he's tried to form against you!

Before you know it, you'll notice that not only is the enemy out of ammunition, but he has also turned and is running away from *you* in terror! That will cause your heart to leap with joy! That's when you need to begin to walk toward those mountains the enemy has told you were so insurmountable. Speak the Word of God to your circumstances and problems until you get right on top of every mountain, and then you tread *on them* as if they were nothing! With God's Word, they are nothing!

Take your authority over Satan! Put him in his place! He's a defeated foe! Then begin to speak God's Word in faith for the blessings you need in your life.

Sad to say, instead of acting in faith in the trials and tests of life, many Christians just wring their hands and cry, "What are we going to do now? Oh, no, God has left us!" Sure, they walk with God and they believe in the Word of God. Many even quote all the right scriptures: "God promises me the victory in Christ," and "I can do all things through Christ who strengthens me." They make all the right faith confessions and quote all the right faith statements. But they're missing it in their *commitment* to God's Word.

That's why so many Christians today are not succeeding at anything they do, and are not receiving their promised blessings from God. They make "faith" statements, but there's no commitment to back up those statements. Therefore, their faith has no substance or backbone to it; every wind of trial sends them spinning in doubt and unbelief.

Christians can make all the faith statements they want to make, but if there's no commitment to God's Word to back up those statements, their faith won't be able to stand up under pressure. What many Christians have failed to realize is that strong faith in God will require something of *you*. It will require a strong commitment *on your part* to God, to His Word, and to His will for your life.

Faith in God and His Word always calls for commitment, because when you believe God's Word — just as these Hebrew children did — you will have to stand for

what you believe. Shadrach, Meshach, and Abednego
believed what the Ten Commandments said — "Thou shalt
have no other gods before Me" so they would not bow to
a graven image (Exod. 20:3,4). But before they could
succeed in God, they had to take a stand for what they
believed in! In order to succeed in God, you will have to
do the same thing!

The same God of Shadrach, Meshach, and Abednego
is your God — if you have accepted Jesus Christ as your
Lord and Savior. And just as they did, you, too, can walk
through any fiery furnace or trial that the devil may throw
your way. The devil can heat that trial fifty times hotter
than usual, but you can *still* walk through it unharmed
because that's what God's Word promises! And when you
come through it victoriously, the devil and all the forces
of hell will have to bow and say there's no God except the
Lord God!

If you want to see men and women with strong faith
and strong commitment, look at the heroes of faith listed
in Hebrews chapter 11. It was said of them that they
refused to give in to the enemy, and because of that they
obtained a good report by their faith (Heb. 11:39). If you
refuse to relinquish your faith in God, you, too, can obtain
a good report. Don't we all want to receive a "good report"
from God for the lives we've lived?

When you know God and walk with Him, there is no
problem that is unsolvable; there is no fear that is unconquerable. Your needs may seem overwhelming at times,
the challenges to your faith may be real, and your faith
may be sorely tested at times. But if you'll put your trust
in God, He'll see to it that you conquer every fear and overcome every problem and obstacle.

You will never reach your full potential in God and your faith will never shine like refined gold if you quit and settle for less than what God has for you. What will you win if you quit? What can you lose by believing God's Word, even in the midst of every trial or test?

Look back over your experiences with God and review the battles God has already brought you through and the victories He has given you. Will God do any less for you in the future?

If you haven't been as victorious as you felt you could have been, you may need to review those commitments you made to God in the past. Ask God to forgive you if you have even *entertained* thoughts of quitting. Determine once again that you want to exercise your faith in God's Word so you can be a success in life. You don't have to quit and you don't have to settle for second best — if you'll develop strong faith in God!

Chapter 4
Faith That Won't Quit!

I am reminded of another account in the Bible of a man who would not give up his faith in God — even in the face of insurmountable obstacles. Mark chapter 10 gives us the account of blind Bartimaeus. We can envision Bartimaeus on the Jericho road clutching his rags and shivering in the cold as he sits begging by the side of the road.

MARK 10:46-52
46 And they came to Jericho: and as he [Jesus] went out of Jericho with his disciples and a great number of people, blind Bartimaeus, the son of Timaeus, sat by the highway side begging.
47 And when he heard that it was Jesus of Nazareth, he began to cry out, and say, Jesus, thou son of David, have mercy on me.
48 And many charged him that he should hold his peace: but he cried the more a great deal, Thou son of David, have mercy on me.
49 And Jesus stood still, and commanded him to be called. And they call the blind man, saying unto him, Be of good comfort, rise; he calleth thee.
50 And he, casting away his garment, rose, and came to Jesus.
51 And Jesus answered and said unto him, What wilt thou that I should do unto thee? The blind man said unto him, Lord, that I might receive my sight.
52 And Jesus said unto him, Go thy way; thy faith hath made thee whole. And immediately he received his sight, and followed Jesus in the way.

Imagine Bartimaeus sitting there by the road, dusty and dirty. I imagine people kicked up dust in his face as they traveled that road to Jericho on their donkeys, horses, camels, and on foot. Picture him as he perhaps sat there rattling an old cup, begging people for money as they passed by.

From the natural standpoint, Bartimaeus had no hope — he had no future; he was a blind beggar, crying out to others just so he could barely get by in life. The word "beggar" carries the connotation of a dirty, dusty, unkempt person clothed with worn and tattered garments. The circumstances of life couldn't get much worse than what Bartimaeus probably experienced. What did he have to hope for? He was probably so helpless that he may have even needed someone to lead him everywhere he went.

In this country, particularly in this day and age, we don't see many beggars. When I was a child, we lived in a suburb of Dallas at one time, and this was before we had all the shopping centers that we have now, so everyone went into town to do their shopping. I can remember going into town as a child, and on many occasions, there sitting on the sidewalk on one of the busiest streets of downtown Dallas, was a blind man begging for food and money. On the corner of one of the busiest thoroughfares of the city, this blind man used to sit day after day begging. He rattled a cup with some pencils in it as people passed by, hoping someone would take a pencil and drop money into the cup.

I imagine that beggar in downtown Dallas was much like blind Bartimaeus. There Bartimaeus sat day after day begging by the side of the Jericho road. He had no hope and no future. He was probably just barely getting enough money to live on from the people who passed by.

In the midst of this dismal hopelessness, all of a sudden Bartimaeus became aware of a commotion in the street. He probably reached out, groping, and grabbed someone's garment close by and asked, "What's going on?" He couldn't see a thing; the only way he knew anything at all was happening was by what he heard and by what others told him.

When a person is blind, his other senses seem to become more keen, especially the sense of hearing. When I was growing up, my grandmother (we called her "Pat's Momma") was blind. She wasn't blind due to a physical ailment; the doctors said it was due to an emotional upheaval which had occurred in her life. (Her husband had run off and left her to raise four children by herself, and the strain of it was just too much for her and she became blind.)

I stayed at her house on many occasions, and I can remember her acute sense of hearing. For instance, I used to sit with her on the back porch during the summertime. All of the windows were open — this was before air conditioners were commonplace — and on hot summer days, we'd have a little fan in the room to try to create a breeze.

My grandmother and I could be sitting on the back porch in the rear of the house, and when someone would drive up to the house, almost without exception, she could tell me who it was.

I remember on one occasion my grandmother and I were visiting on the back porch, when all of a sudden she said, "Son, your daddy just drove up." My dad and mom were out preaching; that's why I was staying with my grandmother. I knew they should still be at their meeting, so I said, "Are you sure? They're not supposed to be here for a while." She said, "I don't know about that; I just know I heard your dad's car out front." And sure enough, it was! Her hearing was so keen, she even knew the sound of each family member's car!

I could be sitting with her on the porch or in the living room with the door open, and as people walked by the house on the sidewalk, before they even came up on the porch, my grandmother would say, "Here comes So-and-so." She knew the footsteps of every one of our relatives, neighbors, and friends, and she could tell you who was approaching before they got to the porch. I'd look out the window or down the steps, and sure enough, she was right every time!

One day I asked her, "How do you know who's coming?" She said, "Everyone has a different walk. You, your dad, and your uncle Dub have a similar stride, but I can tell the difference between the three of you." Because of these experiences with my grandmother, I learned what an acute sense of hearing blind people can have.

Blind Bartimaeus may have had this same ability; his sense of hearing may have been keen and highly developed too. That day on the Jericho road, he could probably hear that something unusual was going on long before Jesus got close to him. He probably fumbled around and grabbed someone who was passing by and demanded, "What's happening? What's going on?" Finally, someone answered him, "Jesus of Nazareth is passing by!"

Can't you just imagine that poor, blind beggar when he heard that news! He was probably sitting on the ground — dust flying all over from the shuffling of the crowd and all the commotion — and then he heard that Jesus of Nazareth was coming his way!

We have to surmise about Bartimaeus' reaction to those words, but I can just imagine him asking, "Isn't Jesus of Nazareth the Man who's healing all those people?

Isn't Jesus the Man they say is anointed of God to do good and to heal all those who are oppressed of the devil? Isn't Jesus of Nazareth the One they call, 'The Wonder Worker'?"

"Yes, it's Jesus Christ, the One who sets men free!"

With the realization that it was *Jesus* who was approaching, I can just see Bartimaeus leap to his feet. He couldn't see anything, but he could hear and he could speak! The Bible says he began to cry out, "Jesus, Thou Son of David, have mercy on me." Immediately those around him began to tell him to sit down and be quiet! *"And many charged him that he should hold his peace..."* (Mark 10:48). But I want you to notice that Bartimaeus refused to quit! He refused to give up! He knew what he wanted from God, and his faith would not take no for an answer. In fact, the more the crowd tried to quench his faith, the more Bartimaeus cried out: *"... but he cried the more a great deal, Thou son of David, have mercy on me"* (v. 48)!

In Texas where I come from, "to cry a great deal more" just means that Bartimaeus began *to yell!* Down in Texas when you're rounding up cattle and you need to get someone's attention "way over yonder" or on the other side of the herd, you yell. And I can imagine that Bartimaeus let out a loud cry because he wanted to get the Master's attention! His faith would not be denied! *Faith always demands a response!* Bartimaeus wanted something from God! He wanted to see!

Faith voices its desires to God — it isn't silent and passive. It demands to be heard in the courts of heaven! The Bible doesn't say that Bartimaeus just sat down quietly and said to himself, *Well, maybe if I'm quiet and*

I just sort of "project" my thoughts to Jesus, He'll come by and touch me and I'll be healed! No, Bartimaeus' faith was not passive. He did not say what we hear so many people in our day saying (and that's why they aren't receiving from God), "Well, *if* it's God's will, Jesus will heal me"!

No! Strong faith won't quit; it refuses to be silent; it won't be denied because it knows God will answer from on High!

Bartimaeus' faith was strong and insistent as he cried out even louder in faith knowing that Jesus would hear him: "JESUS!!! THOU SON OF DAVID!!! HAVE MERCY ON ME!!!" I can just imagine that even the very leaves on the trees were shaken with the power in the Name of Jesus as Bartimaeus cried aloud that Name which is above every name! There's power in Jesus' Name!

But look at the obstacles that stood between Bartimaeus and his prayer being answered. For one thing, in the crowd that met Jesus as He traveled along the Jericho road, I'm sure there were many cold, starchy "religious" people of the day. Because religion adheres strictly to man's traditions instead of embracing an active faith in Jesus, the religious zealots of the day probably could not endure the sound of faith as it came from the lips of Bartimaeus. Religion tries to subdue and altogether extinguish faith, and if there were religious zealots in this crowd, they were probably the very ones who kept telling Bartimaeus, "Hold your peace!" (Mark 10:48).

Religion can be a great obstacle and hindrance to faith, but Bartimaeus determined that *no obstacle* was going to keep him from receiving what he wanted from God! Religion or no religion — no one was going to make Bartimaeus be quiet and lose out on his blessing from God!

That blind beggar had just enough gumption and faith to cry out to Jesus, "Thou Son of David, have mercy on me! I want to see!" God hears the sincere cry of faith!

Now let's picture this scene from Jesus' viewpoint. As Jesus was walking down that dusty Jericho road, all of a sudden He heard His Name being called, and it sounded like a desperate cry. Jesus Christ of Nazareth — His every step ordered by the Holy Spirit from on High — stopped in His tracks when He heard that piercing cry of faith! There was something in that cry — it was a voice of such strong faith and conviction in God's power that it insisted upon being heard! It was a voice filled with faith that would not quit and refused to be silenced!

Bartimaeus' strong faith could not be denied, silenced, or refused. That's the kind of faith that will cause blind eyes to be opened! Bartimaeus was convinced that Jesus could heal him. He was totally, one hundred percent convinced of God's power working on his behalf, and that's faith. He refused to be denied his chance at God's best for his life! It was now or never as far as Bartimaeus was concerned; for all he knew, Jesus might never be passing that way again. Bartimaeus knew this was *his* hour, and he had to take his healing with a violent kind of faith which would not be denied.

Do you have that kind of violent faith which refuses to take no for an answer? It's time you begin to cry out to God with a voice of faith that won't be denied! The cry of faith *will not* be silenced and it *cannot* be quenched. The cry of real faith will never quit or give up! Do not allow the devil to steal from you what rightfully belongs to you by telling you God won't hear your prayer. The Bible says God always hears the cry of the righteous (Ps. 34:15). Put

Satan in his place and all his doubt and unbelief by using the Name of Jesus. Refuse to quit and you can receive what you want from God!

Faith receives an answer from God. Jesus called for Bartimaeus to be brought to Him. *"And Jesus stood still, and commanded him to be called ... "* (v. 49). That same crowd that was trying to silence Bartimaeus a few minutes before began pushing Bartimaeus forward. Although Bartimaeus' blind eyes couldn't see, he could hear the Master's voice. And when Jesus said, "What do you want Me to do for you?" Bartimaeus responded without a moment's hesitation, "I want to see!" Bartimaeus began to rejoice and praise God when he heard Jesus' response: *"... Go thy way; thy faith hath made thee whole ..."* (Mark 10:52). Bartimaeus had every opportunity to quit, but because he refused to give in to the circumstances and the obstacles which had tried to block his way, he went away rejoicing!

As you begin to believe God for the things God has promised you, you will probably have many opportunities to quit because of the problems and obstacles which will try to block your way. You might even hear people try to tell you, "God's promises aren't for us today. They were just for those people who lived back in Jesus' day." You'll also hear the voice of doubt and unbelief which will try to convince you, "God isn't concerned about you. Oh, God exists all right; He is the Supreme Being, but He just isn't interested in mankind." Some theologians would have us believe that. But I don't care who said it — or how many degrees they have behind their names — if it contradicts God's Word, it's wrong! God does care about us; His Word declares it.

1 PETER 5:7
7 Casting all your care upon him; FOR HE CARETH
FOR YOU.

1 PETER 5:7 (*Amplified*)
7 Casting the whole of your care — all your anxieties, all
your worries, all your concerns, once and for all — on Him;
for HE CARES FOR YOU AFFECTIONATELY, and
CARES ABOUT YOU WATCHFULLY.

Bartimaeus received his answer from God. He received
what he wanted from God because he didn't compromise
his faith in God. Let's be sure none of us compromise our
faith and settle for less than God's best for our own lives.
I don't know about you, but I want to receive the very
best God has to offer! I will never compromise! I will go
on to victory because the Word of God declares that
victory in every circumstance belongs to me. If you're a
born-again Christian, victory belongs to you, too, so take
God at His Word!

There is no defeat in faith. All the onslaughts of hell
cannot quench your faith if you have committed yourself
to God. If you live a life pleasing to God and claim what
is rightfully yours through the Word of God, there's no
way you can be defeated!

Chapter 5
Don't Settle for Second Best!

Why do God's people settle for second best? One reason some people settle for second best is that they believe they must compromise because of sins they have committed in the past. They seem to think, *I don't deserve God's best. I've been so bad that if the Lord would just help me out a little bit — that's all I deserve.*

But when a person becomes a new creature in Christ, every sin he's ever committed has been done away with. It's as if that page in his life has been erased because he is recreated and becomes a new creature in Christ. "Behold all things are made new" (2 Cor. 5:17). Everything he did as an "old creature" has been done away with. As a new creature or a new creation in Christ, he deserves God's best because he's been adopted into the family of God. He has become a joint-heir with Jesus Christ (Rom. 8:17).

So many Christians settle for second best when they don't have to. Samson was a man in the Word of God who settled for second best. That great man was a judge of Israel for many years, but he made some mistakes.

You know the story: Samson had been at the pinnacle of success in Israel. The Bible says he judged Israel twenty years. Samson's amazing feats of strength and physical prowess could only be attributed to the power and the anointing of God on his life. The Philistines were terrified by this great man of strength and valor. But then Samson made some mistakes and stumbled morally, and because of that, the enemy discovered the secret to his anointing, and he was stripped of his great strength and power. He fell to the very pit of despair, and became little more than a slave of the Philistines. After all the glory he had won for Israel as the champion of God, his mistakes caused him to miss God's best for his life. His sight was gone and Samson was humbled and brought low in life.

When Samson lost the anointing, he lost the power of God. When that happened, the Philistines were able to take this once powerful man of God captive and make him their slave. They put out his eyes and tied him to a grist-mill where he became nothing more than a mere beast of burden. However, God in His faithfulness never stops listening to the prayers of those who cry out to Him in faith.

That big hulk of a man who was once the hero of Israel was now chained to a gristmill, endlessly — day after day — grinding at a mill. It looked as if Samson's life was going to end in failure even though at one time he had been so mightily used of God. With the anointing of God on Samson's life, it had almost seemed as if nothing was impossible to him.

Under the New Covenant, God's people are born again and the Holy Spirit is tabernacled on the inside of them. But under the Old Testament, men and women were not born again; they did not have a new nature. Therefore, the Holy Spirit did not reside *inside* them, but only *came upon* them so they could perform their God-given task or stand in the office to which God had called them.

Samson was anointed by the Spirit of God to be Israel's deliverer at that particular time, and the Spirit of God would come mightily upon him to perform that task (Judges 13:25; 14:6; 14:19; 15:14). Samson had taken the vow of a Nazarite (Judges 13:5). That vow and his physical strength and prowess were the signs of Samson's anointing and the call that was on his life. But because he defiled himself, he had allowed the enemy to steal the glory of the Lord from him, and now his life looked as if it would end in absolute defeat.

All odds were against Samson. The Philistines were celebrating and worshipping their false gods, jeering and mocking the Lord God Jehovah and making sport of Samson, once God's anointed champion, who was now bound and fettered. But in the midst of the most trying time of his life, as he was walking around in the depths of despair chained to that gristmill Samson cried out to God. He began to talk to God. He made the decision to again call out to God for help and to walk in the anointing of God for help and to walk in the anointing of God once again regardless of the circumstances. He may have rehearsed the commitments he had made to God long ago. We do know that he must have repented because God heard his prayer.

JUDGES 16:21-30
21 ... the Philistines took him, and put out his eyes, and brought him down to Gaza, and bound him with fetters of brass; and he did grind in the prison house.
22 Howbeit the hair of his head began to grow again after he was shaven.
23 Then the lords of the Philistines gathered them together for to offer a great sacrifice unto Dagon their god, and to rejoice: for they said, Our god hath delivered Samson our enemy into our hand.
24 And when the people saw him, they praised their god: for they said, Our god hath delivered into our hands our enemy, and the destroyer of our country, which slew many of us.
25 And it came to pass, when their hearts were merry, that they said, Call for Samson, that he may make us sport. And they called for Samson out of the prison house; and he made

them sport: and they set him between the pillars.

26 And Samson said unto the lad that held him by the hand, Suffer me that I may feel the pillars whereupon the house standeth, that I may lean upon them.

27 Now the house was full of men and women; and all the lords of the Philistines were there; and there were upon the roof about three thousand men and women, that beheld while Samson made sport.

28 And Samson CALLED UNTO THE LORD, and said, O Lord God, remember me, I pray thee, and strengthen me, I pray thee, only this once, O God, that I may be at once avenged of the Philistines for my two eyes.

29 And Samson took hold of the two middle pillars upon which the house stood, and on which it was borne up, of the one with his right hand, and of the other with his left.

30 And Samson said, Let me die with the Philistines. And he bowed himself with all his might; and the house fell upon the lords, and upon all the people that were therein. So the dead which he slew at his death were more than they which he slew in his life.

I can just imagine Samson's heartfelt prayer to God. We do not know for certain, but he may have prayed something like this: "God, please forgive me for my failures. I know I've made a mess of things, but help me now! The devil came at me and tempted me and I fell into his trap, but please give me one more chance to defeat the enemy. I don't want to go out of this life beaten by the enemy; I want to triumph over the enemy to your glory."

You probably know the story: God heard Samson when he cried out to Him, and Samson's strength was once again returned to him. And as Samson grabbed ahold of those huge columns in that house where about three thousand Philistines had gathered to worship their gods, all of a sudden the power and strength of God came upon him once

again. There was a cracking and a groaning as that whole
temple came crashing down and utterly destroyed God's
enemy, the Philistines, who had continually mocked the
Lord God Jehovah and had made sport of one of God's
anointed.

I want you to get this point: Samson was in a desperate
circumstance and in the pit of despair when he made the
decision to once again call upon God to rout the enemy
in his life. He felt that he had made a failure of his life,
and that there was no more hope for him. But he got right
with God, and it was said of Samson that in his death he
was a greater victor than he had been in his life (v. 30).
In fact, Samson's life is recorded in that great passage in
Hebrews 11 which lists God's heroes of faith!

God Turns Failure to Victory!

At one time or another, maybe you have felt as Samson
did — that you've failed in life. But just because you may
have failed and made some mistakes, doesn't mean you
have to compromise and settle for second best in your life.
I'm not encouraging failure. I'm simply saying that if you
have failed in your walk with God, you can confess your
sin and go on and achieve victory in God. First John 1:9
was written for the Christian.

> 1 JOHN 1:9
> 9 If we confess our sins, he is faithful and just to forgive
> us our sins, and to cleanse us from all unrighteousness.

If you've repented and have turned away from sin, God
will hear your prayers. It's not God's plan that you settle

for second best. It's God's plan that you make a commitment to Him and then live by that commitment so He can prosper you in every area of life.

The Word of God says that our heavenly Father is a loving God and He cares about us. His thoughts are above our thoughts and His ways are above our ways. He is not going to hold our mistakes against us if we have repented (Isa. 55:7-9). How many of you parents keep on holding it against your children when they've failed or made mistakes? That doesn't mean we don't discipline and correct our children when they make mistakes because we want what's best for them. But when they repent, we forgive them. God is the same way. As a loving Father, He wants what's best for us. He disciplines us, but He doesn't do it with sickness and disease. Who ever heard of a loving father breaking his children's legs or making his children sick so he could teach them a lesson? That's not the God I know!

God's Waiting Just for You

For some of you, it may seem as if you're down for the count and about to be defeated. Maybe you've even asked yourself, *What's the use?* But I want you to know that if you won't quit, your success is not far off. It's just waiting to come to you because God promises in His Word that we will always triumph in Christ (2 Cor. 2:14). The only condition to always triumphing is staying *in Christ.* That means staying in faith and staying in obedience! Don't quit. You've come this far, and your faith will see you through. Rely on God and keep on going in faith!

Faith knows no defeat. In God there is no problem that

is unsolvable; there is no fear that is unconquerable if you'll stand true to God. Yes, your needs may be many, and your perplexities great; your trials may seem overwhelming at times, and you may be facing problems that you don't know how to solve. Some of you may not even know where your next dollar is coming from or how you are going to pay your bills. But I challenge and admonish you to dare to believe the Word of God. God knows everything you're facing, and He knows how to bring you out of every problem.

There's never been a problem that has been placed in the hands of God which has not been completely solved and resolved. But you must put your problems in His hands and not try to solve them yourself. There has never been a problem or a circumstance that has been placed in the hands of God by a child of His who was trusting and believing in His Word, that has not received heaven's best.

I encourage you to stand firm in your faith in God! If God could take care of that vast host of Israelites as they marched across the desert on their way to the Promised Land, He can take care of us even in this day of adversity we live in. If God could take care of the prophet Elijah and tell him exactly where to go in the midst of famine in order to be sustained by a little widow woman, I believe He can take care of us! We serve a God who is bigger than this world's economic situation. God can sustain us no matter what circumstances may come upon the earth.

God Has a Way Out!

When my wife and I were just starting out in the ministry, we faced some trying times financially. Each month we'd figure up our income and then we'd figure our disbursements, and our disbursements were more than our income.

But we stood firm in our faith in God and committed our financial burdens to God. We prayed, "God, we've chosen You and we've chosen to walk in Your path and to do what You want us to do. We've done all we know to do, so we just commit this problem to You. We know that You will take care of us according to Your Word." Then we just stood on God's Word and committed our needs to God. It may sound amazing, but at the end of the month every one of our bills was paid and there was money left over! To this day I don't know how that happened; as far as I could tell we had no extra income. All I know is that when we committed our needs and burdens to God, He took care of the problem!

I challenge you to stay faithful to whatever God has called you to do so that you can receive the victory in every circumstance in your life. What will you win if you quit? You have everything to gain by trusting God. If you've made mistakes and you think you've made such a mess of your life that it's too late — if you have sincerely repented — it's *never* too late with God!

Yes, Satan will always try to tempt you to become discouraged. He may even try to throw at you some of the very same trials and temptations that you've already faced before in your life. How do I know? Because I know the devil's tactics. The Bible says he goes around as a roaring lion seeking whom he may devour (1 Peter 5:8). Yes, you may be facing some tremendous challenges. You may even be facing some physical challenges of sickness or disease in your body. But did you know that it's not up to God whether you are a success or a failure in life — it's up to you! You hold the key to your own success. Your redemption is already made sure and declared in God's Word. Now you just need to appropriate God's Word for yourself.

What do you choose to do? Do you choose to believe what other people say about God or do you choose to take God at His Word? Do you choose to believe the symptoms the devil is trying to put on your body, or do you choose to believe God means what He says in His Word: "By His stripes you are healed" (Isa. 53:5; 1 Peter 2:24; Matt. 8:17)? What about the economy? Do you choose to believe what the world's economists say is going to happen, or do you choose to believe that God will take care of you? Do you believe God was being truthful when He said He would supply all of your needs according to His riches in glory by Christ Jesus, and that you can do all things through Christ who strengthens you (Phil. 4:19; Phil. 4:13)? Do you choose to crumble in fear or to believe that ". . . *the Lord is the strength of my life; of whom shall I be afraid?*" (Ps. 27:1).

Do you choose to believe what Jesus said in Mark 9:23: "All things are possible to him that believes?" What about Luke 18:27: *"The things which are impossible with men are possible with God"*? Or are you going to throw up your hands and say, "Well, I thought God was going to move on my behalf, but I guess He isn't"? Are you just going to go on letting the devil try to put torment, fear, and lack in your life, or are you going to rebuke him and say, "Satan, Jesus already defeated you, and you don't have any power or authority over me!"

You see, God's Word and the Name of Jesus are all

you need to put the devil in his place. Faith and obedience to God's Word and the Name of Jesus are all you need to unlock the storehouses of heaven so that innumerable blessings can be poured out upon you. We're not talking about the word of a man; we're talking about the Word of *God!*

Some Christians have never fully trusted in God. They say, "Well, I'll pray about it, but if God doesn't come through for me, I'll try something else." They make their own way of escape. But God promised us in His Word that *He* would always provide a way of escape out of any trial for the righteous (1 Cor. 10:13).

When Christians try to make their own way of escape or deliverance instead of relying on God, they're building failure into their lives. They are going to have to learn to live by faith daily. Those Christians who are successful have learned to stand on God's Word regardless of circumstances. Sometimes when I've been standing in faith about a situation, I've told God, "God if I fail, You are going to have to fail first, because I'm standing on Your Word and I know Your Word will never fail!"

Complacent Christians Fail To Receive God's Best

It seems that many Christians come to the point in their Christian walk where they are willing to compromise their values and their goals. "Well, I've experienced some success, so I guess I'll just be satisfied. It doesn't look as if everything God has promised me will come to pass, so I'll just be satisfied with what I have."

You can have that attitude and still be a child of the King. God will allow you to settle for second best if you want. It's not what *He* wants for you, but if that's what you want, you can have it.

We read about people in the Word of God who have chosen second best when they could have had something better. For example, the children of Israel settled for less than God's best when they chose to have a king (1 Sam. 8:1-22). God didn't want them to have a king; it wasn't His best for them. He knew the consequences they would face if they chose to have a king, but they wanted to live as the heathen nations did and to be like them.

Well, that wasn't God's best and He told them so. But He didn't disown the children of Israel just because they were willing to settle for second best. They were still His children and He still took care of them. God finally let them have a king, and they soon realized that having a king wasn't quite what they thought it would be. God tried to tell them, but they wouldn't listen; they settled for second best.

You belong to the King of kings. You don't have to settle for second best in life! Don't be satisfied with a "just-get-by" attitude. God wants so much more for His people.

The Word of God promises us so much more than just "getting by." When God promised us in His Word that He would supply all of our needs according to *His* riches in glory, that doesn't mean that we would *just get by*. He has promised to deliver us out of all of our trials and all of our temptations. That doesn't just mean *some* of them. That means *all* of them. If we had to settle for just barely getting by in life, that would mean God was only willing to deliver us out of some of our trials. That would also mean He wasn't able to supply us with His riches in glory. But that's not what His Word declares! Let's dare to take

God at His Word!

I want you to realize that the devil will always try to convince you to compromise and settle for second best in your life. I will never forget an incident that happened in the 1950s at a healing meeting my dad held in California. I was with him at that meeting. There was a huge stage or platform in the church where the meeting was held. Since there was very little room anywhere else to pray for the people, we had the people who needed prayer for healing, come up on the platform. One of the people who came forward for prayer was a little old lady who was doubled over with arthritis. Leaning heavily on a cane, she came hobbling across the stage.

My dad said to her, "What do you need from the Lord, Sister?"

"Eh?"

"What do you need from the Lord?"

"What did you say?"

My dad shouted, "What do you need from the Lord?"

"Oh," she said, "I can't hear. I need to hear!"

He shouted, "Oh, you need healing for your ears?"

"Yes!"

My dad put his fingers in her ears and prayed for her, and her ears popped open. Then he walked about twenty-five feet away from her and said in a low voice, "Jesus." She answered, "Jesus." She could hear just as well as he could!

Everyone in that place began to praise the Lord. That little old lady rejoiced greatly because her ears were healed. Then she turned around and began to hobble back across the platform, still doubled over with arthritis. My dad said, "Wait a minute, Sister! What about that walking stick?

Don't you need something else from the Lord?"

"No," she answered. "I can get by with this arthritis, but I couldn't get by with those deaf ears," and she walked off the platform and went and sat down.

God was well able to heal both the arthritis and her deafness, but she stopped short of her victory! She settled for second best.

Faith knows that God is a God who's more than enough! Dare to come boldly to God to obtain your needs met in full! God will not disappoint the one who asks in faith believing — taking Him at His Word!

Chapter 6
Fight the Good Fight of Faith!

We've said that God will meet our needs if we come to Him and ask Him *in faith*. But we must also realize that there will be those times in our lives when we will have to fight *the good fight of faith*. We will have to believe God and trust in His Word. The Bible says in First Timothy 6:12 that we are to fight the good fight of faith. There will be those times when we will have to stand our ground and not quit even when it looks like we're going down for the count. But don't quit! God will cause you to be victorious if you will believe His Word and not give up.

You know, it's one thing in the natural if you quit in a fight. But when you embark upon this spiritual fight and you quit in the middle of a fight, the consequences can be extremely sobering; it could mean *life* or *death*.

So stay in the fight of faith! Yes, you may lose a round or two in the fight of faith. The devil may take you by surprise, but just because you lose a few rounds doesn't mean you lose the whole fight. You may come away from that first round or two with a black eye and a bloody nose until you learn how to stand on the Word for your victory. But just because the devil gets in a couple of good licks — maybe a right cross and a left hook, and you may be staggering a little or bouncing off the ropes — that doesn't mean he's won the whole fight!

If you'll put your trust in the Word of God instead of on what you can do or see in the natural, you'll be ready for the next round. Get into God's Word and get your spiritual "muscles" built up and then go back out there and meet the enemy in the center of the ring. Wind up and deliver him a strong, sharp uppercut punch with the Word of God, and knock him right out of that circumstance he's been holding over your head for so long!

If you're going to whip the devil in every circumstance of life, you must have the attitude that you refuse to quit and that the devil will not defeat you or take anything that legally belongs to you again! Remember, in Christ, if you'll stay faithful to God's Word, you are assured of the victory in every circumstance.

However, you are the one who is going to have to make up your mind to win the fight of faith when the circumstances get rough round about you. When everything looks dark and hopeless, and there's no victory in sight, what are you going to trust? The circumstances? Your fears? Or the Word of God!

When the wind of adversity is blowing and the devil's threats are howling round about you like a mighty storm in your life; when it looks like your ship is about to go under from the waves that have risen up against it — that's exactly when you're going to have to be determined to fight the fight of faith! If you're going to see victory, you're going to have to make up your mind to stick with the fight of faith no matter what — regardless of what circumstances *look* like.

There are too many Christians who are falling for the devil's lies. When they are just about to achieve victory, the devil starts blowing and huffing and puffing — telling them they'll never win, and they get scared off and back away from the victory. Instead of pressing on in faith, they begin to say, "Well, I guess I might as well give up! God isn't going to answer me this time." And they quit and lay their faith down, and that's as far as they ever go. They never take another step or make another advance to gain the territory God has already promised them. I didn't say they weren't saved; I just said they aren't advancing toward the blessings God has for them because they've listened to the devil's lies and they've given up the fight of faith.

I don't believe in quitting! I don't think God believes in quitting either. If you'll read the Word of God, you'll see that the people God used were those who refused to quit! They weren't people who were necessarily any braver, wiser, or smarter than we are. They were just people with a tenacity and determination of faith who wouldn't take no for an answer!

Don't be satisfied with second best from God! But on the other hand, don't be upset with yourself if you lose a round or two either, because condemnation is the devil's way to try to get you down. Losing a round or two in a fight is not the whole fight! Make up your mind: "I am determined to follow God's plan for my life. I will not turn aside from following Jesus no matter what!" And if you're out there in the midst of the fight when the last bell rings and you've been faithful to what God has told you to do, you're going to be wearing a victor's crown!

There's another reason we shouldn't quit fighting the good fight of faith.

HEBREWS 11:32-34
32 And what shall I more say? for the time would fail me to tell of Gedeon [Gideon], and of Barak, and of Samson, and of Jephthae; of David also, and Samuel, and of the prophets:
33 Who through faith subdued kingdoms, wrought righteousness, obtained promises, stopped the mouths of lions,

> 34 Quenched the violence of fire, escaped the edge of the
> sword, out of weakness were made strong, waxed valiant
> in fight, turned to flight the armies of the aliens.

The writer of Hebrews is saying here that so many mighty acts of righteousness have been wrought by mighty men and women of God because they refused to let go of their faith in God, that he'd run out of time trying to tell us about them all! These powerful men and women of faith kept their faith in God stalwart and strong in the face of the fire, in the face of the lion, and in the face of every obstacle they encountered in life! If they could do it, so can we, because God is still the same God now as He was then! What He did for those who trusted Him in the past, He'll do for us today!

A Great Cloud of Witnesses

HEBREWS 12:1
1 Wherefore seeing we also are compassed about with so
great a cloud of witnesses, let us lay aside every weight,
and the sin which doth so easily beset us, and let us run
with patience the race that is set before us.

In this passage of Scripture, Paul uses the image of the Greek Olympiad — the ancient Greek games — as an illustration so we can relate to what he is talking about. In ancient Greece, the athletes who competed in this race wore heavy weights on their legs and arms, and armor-like plates on their bodies as they were engaged in training to prepare for the Greek games. They did this so their bodies would be accustomed to rigorous discipline and hardship, so they would have the endurance, condition, and stamina they would need in the actual contest — the Greek games.

When it came time for the race or the competition in the actual games, those athletes laid aside all those heavy weights. Without all those weights, it seemed as if their bodies were almost weightless, movement seemed effortless, and physical strength and endurance was mightily increased. The stands would be full of cheering spectators watching the athletes as they ran their various races and competed in their great trials of strength and endurance.

Paul uses this imagery of the Greek games as a picture or a type of the Christian running the race of life. He's also saying that we are compassed about with a great cloud of witnesses just as these Greek athletes were compassed about with thousands of spectators cheering them from the stands. In fact, one translation of this verse says, "Wherefore seeing that we are standing on the playing field with a grandstand full of witnesses, let us lay aside the weights that would try to entangle us." I can just imagine that great cloud of witnesses — Peter, Paul, Moses, Abraham — the great patriarchs of old and the whole host of our heavenly family — watching from the balustrades of heaven. Our loved ones who have gone home to be with the Lord are there in that company, too, cheering us on to victory.

When thoughts of defeat are racing through your mind, remember this scripture in Hebrews. Remember that great cloud of witnesses cheering you on to victory: "Come on, you can make it! The Word says you're more than a conqueror." And be encouraged to run your race with patience! Sometimes I think about that great cloud of witnesses and it just spurs me on to victory! But in this race

you must also realize that you are going to have to fight
the fight of faith. Refuse to give up on the promises God
has given you in His Word! Being strong in faith means
that you believe that what God has promised you, He is
able to perform (Rom. 4:20,21).

I can relate to this image of a great cloud of witnesses
cheering from the grandstands because I used to run track.
And I will never forget one incident in particular that
occurred when I was attending school in Oregon. The
school I attended had never had a track team before, but
some of us decided we wanted to run track, so we asked
the history teacher to be our coach and we formed a track
team.

We formed the track team, all right, but it just seemed
as if every circumstance imaginable stood in our way. The
first time we ever ran as a team, everyone laughed at us
because we were four ragtag boys from a small unknown
school who didn't even have proper uniforms or equipment.
We were wearing borrowed jerseys from the basketball
team, none of our track shoes matched, we didn't have
proper equipment or even a trainer to go with us to the
state track meet. In fact, we didn't even have a baton to
pass in the relay race! We had to run with a sawed-off
broom handle! We couldn't afford one of the shiny metal
batons that everyone else used in track meets, so finally
one day in desperation I found an old broom, sawed it off,
rounded off the edges so there wouldn't be any splinters,
and that's what we used for a baton! Talk about an opportunity to quit! We had every opportunity to quit before
we even got started!

Back in those days, we ran on cinder tracks. We didn't
have tar on running tracks as tracks have on them now.

I was running the second leg of the 880 relay, and I had
drawn the outside lane. The runner who was favored to
beat me was running right alongside of me in the next
track. There were eight lanes on that track, and since I
was running on the outside lane, I was out there in front
of everyone in the staggered start.

The coach who called the start of the race looked down
at me and in front of everyone else said, "Son, you're running with the big boys today. Be sure you don't change
lanes and get over into the other runner's lane because
these guys will run you over!" How humiliating! That was
like saying "sic 'em" to a dog! When he said that I determined to myself, *I'll show him. What does he mean, talking like I've already lost the race before I've even started!*

I'll never forget this incident because if I just listened
to circumstances and to what everyone else said about it,
I would have quit! I not only had an excuse *to quit,* I had
an excuse *to fail.* If the team lost that race I could have
just said to myself and to everyone else, "Well, I was running with the big boys, and I just couldn't make it. After
all, I'm just from a small-town school no one's ever heard
of. How could I ever hope to win, running against these
guys!" But instead I told myself, *You're not going to quit;
you're going to win!* I purposed in my heart that I was
going to give it my best — and that I would not give up
and be a quitter. I told the guys on my team, "When you
give me the baton, I want the opponent who's running in
the track next to me to be at least five yards ahead of me
because I'm going to show him! I'm going to beat him."

This was the only race I ever ran that my dad was able
to attend because he was out in the field ministry preaching so much of the time. That's one reason I will never

forget this race. When that coach said, "Runners take your mark. Get set. Go!" The runners were off! I remember when I took that baton from my teammate who ran the first leg, the runner in the track next to me was already ahead of me, just like I wanted him to be. I took off running as hard and as fast as I could.

As we ran around that track, I'll never forget that final curve as we approached the straightaway in front of the grandstands. As we were coming off that curve and I was approaching the straightaway, I could see my dad in the grandstands hanging out over the track cheering me on. As I got a little closer, I could hear him yelling, "Ken, you'd better run, he's catching you. Run!" I was already running with all my strength; I didn't think there was any way I could run any faster. But somehow I reached down inside of me and found new strength, and I ran that last distance with a final burst of speed. I looked down the track to where the next runner was waiting for me to hand him the baton, and I ran as fast as I could. When I got in front of the grandstand, I passed the baton to him. I hadn't heard any other runners beside me, so I turned around to see where everyone else was, and I was twenty yards in front of every other runner on the track!

People had laughed at us before the starting gun sounded, but when all was said and done, we were the ones who were standing in the middle of that track with the first place ribbon!

That incident taught me a lot about persevering and not quitting. Yes, this is a small incident compared to some of the things you may be facing in your life right now. But the principle of persevering when all odds are against you screaming at you to quit is still the same: In order to win, you can't quit! And to a teenaged boy, this was an important lesson to learn early in life about not giving up.

You see, I could have quit when every obstacle blocked my way. I could have given up when that coach said there was no way a small-town boy like me could hope to run against the big boys and win. I had every opportunity to quit, but I refused to give up in spite of all the difficulties we had to face.

I refused to quit! You'll need to have that same kind of attitude if you're going to stop the devil in every contest in your life too. Persevering faith is the only thing that will take you through life because the devil will always try to convince you that you can't make it — that there is no way for you to succeed in life. And the devil will always try to take from you what legally belongs to you.

> **JOHN 10:10**
> 10 The thief cometh not, but for to steal, and to kill, and to destroy: I am come that they might have life, and that they might have it more abundantly.

If you'll make up your mind that you refuse to quit, and if you'll not allow the devil to defeat you, you will come out a winner in every area of your life and you'll be the one standing in the victor's circle!

Run the Christian Race for God's Glory

In my mind's eye, I can see the same thing happening as I run this Christian race. The enemy is always there to try to tell me there's no way I can ever hope to win in life. But there's also a cloud of witnesses, the Bible says, who are ever cheering me on: "Come on! You can make it! Run the race for God! Don't give up now; don't quit now! The victory is yours!"

And as I'm running this race, I'm continually quoting God's Word and that sustains me: "I'm more than a conqueror in Christ Jesus" (Rom. 8:37). "Greater is He that is in me than he that is in the world" (1 John 4:4). "Thanks be unto God who always causes me to triumph in Christ" (2 Cor. 2:14).

Those Christians who know how to run this race for God *by faith,* are choking Satan to death with the dust from their heels as they fly down their course in victory. Maybe the devil has outrun you and defeated you in your race at one time or another. Don't let that deter you! You can overcome him if you'll just get back in the race and start to run again. Run with patience and run by the grace of the Lord Jesus Christ. Always keep in mind that the devil is a defeated foe! Jesus has won the victory over him at the Cross of Calvary! And encourage yourself, because the Bible says that if you're faithful, there's a crown waiting for you on the other side in glory!

If you've been contemplating just giving up and quitting, or if you've even slowed down to a walk, ask God to forgive you. Turn to Him again, and ask Him for renewed strength. Put your sights again on the course God has set for you, and be diligent to run your race so you can receive your reward. If you're born again, you've begun the race, and there's no stopping for you until Jesus Christ comes in the clouds of glory. Then and only then will you cross the finish line. Then and only then should you quit!

I realize many of you may feel weak in faith; your feet may be hurting and your sides may be aching from the exertion of running this race. The devil would like to make it *so* convenient for you to stop and sit down a while. He'll try to tell you to stop running — to give up the race. Or he may try to whisper to you, "Why don't you stay out of the race, *just for a while.*" But if you do, you'll lose every inch of ground that it's taken you months or maybe even years to gain! No, with your faith, press on in the race! Take what belongs to you because of who you are in Christ! You're a victor in Christ Jesus and you are more than a conqueror!

God's Invitation to *You*

HEBREWS 4:16
16 Let us therefore come boldly unto the throne of grace, that we may obtain mercy, and find grace to help in time of need.

You're going to have to come boldly to the throne of grace, and boldly receive what God has for you. You can't approach the throne of grace with the attitude, *Well, God, here I am. Maybe you can help me.* No, you've got to approach God's throne with boldness and confidence in your heart that God is able and willing to help you. God has whatever you might need, because He is an ever-present help in time of trouble.

PSALM 46:1
1   God is our refuge and strength, a very present help in trouble.

Receive what God has already promised you *by faith,* because the enemy will try to keep you from realizing those things already belong to you. If you don't realize God's blessings already belong to you, you won't be able to appropriate your inheritance by faith! This is one of the ways Satan will try to keep you from receiving what has been promised to you in Christ.

Satan will also try to prevent you from receiving what legally belongs to you by giving you every excuse why *you* can't have your prayers answered. He'll craftily try to tell you every reason why you shouldn't come to God's throne, and why you don't deserve what God has for you. He'll give you every reason why God's promise to you should *not* be fulfilled in your life, and why it is impossible for God's Word to come to pass for you.

But I can give you unlimited reasons why everything God has told you *should* come to pass for you — beginning with the One who is unlimited — the Lord Jesus Christ Himself! Jesus has already won your full inheritance for you, and it's all waiting for you to appropriate it by faith! Therefore, come to the throne boldly with great confidence to receive what you need from God!

The Press of Faith

In Bible days women were not as free to mix in public gatherings as they are today. Have you ever noticed, for example, that when crowds were numbered in the New Testament, men were the only ones counted? Women and children were not mentioned. And according to Jewish Law, women were not to be in public gatherings if they were unclean; that is, for example, in the case of a woman who had an issue of blood (Lev. 15:25).

However, we read in the Bible about a woman with an

issue of blood who in coming to Jesus defied the customs and the culture of her times because she had such confidence in the healing power of God. She was confident that one touch from the Master would heal her.

MARK 5:25-34

25 And a certain woman, which had an issue of blood twelve years,

26 And had suffered many things of many physicians, and had spent all that she had, and was nothing bettered, but rather grew worse,

27 When she had heard of Jesus, came in the press behind, and touched his garment.

28 For she said, If I may touch but his clothes, I shall be whole.

29 And straightway the fountain of her blood was dried up; and she felt in her body that she was healed of that plague.

30 And Jesus, immediately knowing in himself that virtue had gone out of him, turned him about in the press, and said, Who touched my clothes?

31 And his disciples said unto him, Thou seest the multitude thronging thee, and sayest thou, Who touched me?

32 And he looked round about to see her that had done this thing.

33 But the woman fearing and trembling, knowing what was done in her, came and fell down before him, and told him all the truth.

34 And he said unto her, Daughter, thy faith hath made thee whole; go in peace, and be whole of thy plague.

I want you to notice that this crowd was pressing upon Jesus from all sides so that Jesus' disciples were amazed at His question, "Who touched Me?" Yet in all that throng of people who were closing in around Jesus, this one little amazing woman was able to reach Jesus with the *touch of faith!* Many touched him, but she was the only one the Bible records who touched Him in faith! We know that she had an issue of blood, so she may have been physically weak or sickly at the time. Yet in spite of every obstacle, this woman accomplished what no one else in that crowd was able to do — to touch Jesus *in faith* — and walk away healed.

One obstacle we know this woman had to overcome was the obstruction of the crowd that pressed in upon Jesus on every side. She may have had to elbow her way past people, push her way in, or perhaps even crawl on her hands and knees in order to reach Jesus. Yes, just as you and I do, she had obstacles to overcome, but she didn't stop short of her goal just because she had some barriers in her way. She knew what she wanted from God and she was determined to get it! And it was her strong, persevering faith that caused her to succeed.

Plead Your Case to God

I want you to notice something else. This woman did not depend on anyone else to plead her case for her to Jesus. She didn't go around asking others to do her praying for her, nor did she try to solicit the help of others so she could get to Jesus. No, she went herself, and she used her own faith to get what she wanted from God.

There are some Christians who will always remain baby Christians because every time something happens, they get on the phone and call a prayer group or call their pastor or Sister Jones down the street to pray for them. But, remember, no one is as concerned about *you* as *you* are!

There is no one who can plead your case before God like you can. Oh, others can pray for you all right. But when it comes right down to it, you're the one who can plead your case most effectively before God because you're the one in the middle of the circumstances, and you know what you need from God. Learn to plead your own case to God. Otherwise, you'll never grow in prayer, and you'll always be dependent upon others to go to God for you.

Another interesting thought about this woman was that she was not afraid to come to God for help. She didn't hang back from coming to God with her need. She wasn't intimidated by the circumstances or even her sickness because that's not what she was looking at! She had her eyes fixed solely on Jesus! Some Christians are so intimidated by the devil or are so overwhelmed by their circumstances that they don't come to God. But in order to get their prayers answered, they are going to have to put all that aside and just focus on Jesus and what His Word promises so they can get what they want from God! That's the secret; keeping the focus of your eyes on God!

Another key element in this woman's success was that she came to Jesus *ready* to receive. Therefore, when she touched Jesus, virtue went out of Him and she was healed. Then Jesus said something interesting to her: "... *Daughter, thy faith hath made thee whole* ..." (v. 34). Jesus didn't say it was *His* faith that had made her whole; He said it was *her* faith that had made her whole. Jesus could have said that to anyone else in that crowd if they'd had that same kind of tenacious faith, but as far as the Bible records, no one else did. As far as the Bible records, this woman was the only one who got her needs met! She wasn't a quitter!

A quitter never wins and a winner never quits! The person who succeeds in God does not know the meaning of the word "quit." On the other hand, a person who fails does not know the meaning of the word "persevere." This woman with the issue of blood was the only one who persevered and received what she needed from God! So can you!

Chapter 7
Persistent Faith

We saw that the woman with the issue of blood had persistent faith even in the face of all obstacles, and that's why she was the only one out of that whole crowd who walked away healed. You see, persistent faith is tenacious. It doesn't let go of the desired goal no matter what Satan may try to throw in its way, and no matter what obstacles may have to be overcome; persistent faith keeps on believing God regardless of circumstances. Persistent faith fights the good fight of faith.

In studying persistent faith, we also need to look at the biblical account of the man taken with palsy. This account of the man who was lowered through the ceiling of a roof by four others is a rather dramatic account of persistent faith — faith that just won't take no for an answer and won't give up no matter what the obstacles are!

LUKE 5:17-26

17 And it came to pass on a certain day, as he [Jesus] was teaching, that there were Pharisees and doctors of the law sitting by, which were come out of every town of Galilee, and Judaea, and Jerusalem: and the power of the Lord was present to heal them.

18 And, behold, men brought in a bed a man which was taken with a palsy: and they sought means to bring him in, and to lay him before him.

19 And when they could not find by what way they might bring him in because of the multitude, they went upon the housetop, and let him down through the tiling with his couch in the midst before Jesus.

20 And when he saw THEIR FAITH, he said unto him, Man, thy sins are forgiven thee.

21 And the scribes and the Pharisees began to reason, say-ing, Who is this which speaketh blasphemies? Who can for-give sins, but God alone?
22 But when Jesus perceived their thoughts, he answer-ing said unto them, What reason ye in your hearts?
23 Whether is easier, to say, Thy sins be forgiven thee; or to say, Rise up and walk?
24 But that ye may know that the Son of man hath power upon earth to forgive sins, (he said unto the sick of the palsy,) I say unto thee, Arise, and take up thy couch, and go into thine house.
25 And immediately he rose up before them, and took up that whereon he lay, and departed to his own house, glorify-ing God.
26 And they were all amazed, and they glorified God, and were filled with fear, saying, We have seen strange things to day.

Persistent faith receives what it needs from God; it refuses to be deterred by obstacles that may be in the way. Also, notice that those with persistent faith will receive when others do not. This house where Jesus was teaching the Word was filled with people, including Pharisees and doctors of the law. So many people were gathered to hear Jesus that the Bible says people were even pressing about the door. The Bible also says, "... *the power of the Lord was present to heal them* [ALL]" (v. 17).

The power of God was available to heal every single person in that house, but only *one* man was healed, and he wasn't even in the house! Why was he healed when no one else was?

Let's look at this same account in Mark. It brings out more of the thought of corporate faith.

MARK 2:2-5
2 And straightway many were gathered together,

> insomuch that there was no room to receive them, no, not
> so much as about the door: and he preached the word unto
> them.
> 3   And they come unto him, bringing one sick of the palsy,
> WHICH WAS BORNE OF FOUR.
> 4   And when they could not come nigh unto him for the
> press, they uncovered the roof where he was: and when they
> had broken it up, they let down the bed wherein the sick
> of the palsy lay.
> 5   When Jesus saw THEIR FAITH, he said unto the sick
> of the palsy, Son, thy sins be forgiven thee.

Here was a man who couldn't even get in the house, and yet he was the only one who was healed! We can see that the man with palsy *demonstrated* his faith. After all, he allowed himself to be carried up to that housetop and lowered down in front of Jesus! How many sick people would let themselves be carried up to a rooftop and be lowered down on a stretcher in order to be healed? When you're sick, it would take faith just to allow yourself to be carried up to a rooftop, let alone to be dropped down through the roof on a stretcher!

Then, too, it would also take faith on the part of those who carried him up to that rooftop! So it wasn't just the man's faith that Jesus commended. Jesus also commended the faith of the four who carried the man and lowered him through the ceiling. The Bible says when Jesus *saw their* faith, He told the man sick with palsy to get up off his bed and walk (vv. 5,9). That's an interesting comment, because faith isn't visible, is it? But the *actions* that faith arouse are visible! We could say it this way: "When Jesus saw their *act* of faith, He said, 'Take up your bed and walk,' and the man got up off his stretcher and went home healed"!

This man and his four companions refused to quit! When presented with an obstacle to their faith — a deterrent — they simply went around it! That man on the stretcher and the four who carried him could have given up when they saw the crowd of people closed in around the door of that house where Jesus was preaching the Word. They could have said, "Well, we might as well go home; this is impossible. Let's not even try." And that sick man would have been carried back home just as sick as he ever was.

But they didn't give up; they persisted in their faith. Also, when they couldn't get into the house, they could have said something we often hear people in our day and age say, "Well, I guess it just wasn't the Lord's will after all." That's the way a lot of people determine the Lord's will — by the circumstance. But the Lord's will is not determined by the circumstances we face in life. God's will is already declared and set forth in His Word, and it includes healing!

I imagine it was fairly easy to take the tiles off the roof of that particular type of house. But, on the other hand, I imagine it was a little unnerving for those who were in the house listening to Jesus preach and teach the Word to all of a sudden hear the tiles of the roof being pulled off! Can you imagine how the man who *owned* the house felt as those four men were tearing up his roof!

But the important point is that when these five men were confronted with an obstacle, they didn't just give up; they did something about it! When they couldn't get to Jesus, their faith wasn't deterred — they just went another way. The Bible says that God will always provide a way of escape. It took some faith to move that obstacle — to

climb up on that roof and to lower that sick man down
into the house! And then it took some faith on the part
of the man who was sick with palsy too, because not only
was he already bedfast, but one false step as his friends
were carrying him up to the roof, and he could have been
worse off than he was before!

Just as a side thought, this also gives us a picture of
what united faith or corporate faith can accomplish. Here
are five people, the man sick of the palsy and the four who
carried him, and all of them have one common goal — to
get to Jesus so the man on the stretcher can be healed.
They were unified in purpose, in goal, and in action to get
the job done. After all, if they hadn't been in absolute
unity, they probably would have just *dumped* that poor
man through the ceiling! And here the poor fellow was
already bedfast; he couldn't walk. But if the men who
lowered him down through the ceiling hadn't been in unity,
he would have been in *pitiful* shape by the time he hit the
ground!

There's a lesson in this for us. To do anything for God
corporately, you're going to have to be in unity — unity
of purpose, unity of goal, and unity of action. In fact, you'll
find in reading through the Acts of the Apostles that the
Bible continually talks about the apostles being in unity
or in one accord. Every time the disciples were in unity,
the power of God was in such manifestation that in one
place it says the very house where they prayed was shaken
(Acts 4:31).

The Bible says that without faith it is impossible to
please God. Persistent faith wins favor with God; it pleases
God! The prayer of unity wins favor with God! This man
was healed, not because his faith or the faith of his

companions was any greater than yours or mine, but because they *persisted* in their faith in spite of obstacles, and they were agreed in purpose. They wouldn't let go of their faith!

That man was the only one who walked away healed that day because he refused to be defeated by his *circumstances.* At any time, he could have told those other men, "This is too hard. Take me home!" but he didn't. He refused to quit and give in when things didn't go just exactly as he thought they should. He refused to accept failure as part of his thinking, so when confronted with an obstacle, he just went around it! His attitude was, *I've come to succeed! I've come to Jesus to get my needs met, and my needs will be met! I've come to receive from God and I will not be defeated!* Therefore, he received what he needed from God.

So many times in the ministry we see people come to meetings, and in five seconds they want to get everything from God there is — the whole dose of God's blessings — and then leave. It doesn't always work that way. Sometimes we have *to persist* in our faith, not because God is withholding from us, but because we have an enemy who is arrayed against us.

Look at this man on the stretcher. This account gives us a biblical example of the persistence of faith. He didn't receive his healing easily. You think it wasn't difficult being carried up on a housetop on a stretcher — not just for him but for the four who had to carry him! They had to push past some obstacles before this man received his healing. You might have to persist in your faith, too, and just keep hanging on to God's Word, even when it doesn't look as if the Word is working for you.

Why do we sometimes have to persist in our faith? Because although the healing power of God is free and available to all, as are all of God's blessings, the enemy will try to throw every obstacle in our way to keep us from receiving what God has for us.

Keep Your Eyes on the Goal

When you make a commitment in your faith to believe God for what He has promised you, you're going to have to be one hundred percent dedicated in your commitment if you are ever going to succeed. You can't stop half way. You won't be able to quit and be satisfied with the status quo — even when you reach a plateau where you feel comfortable. No, you have to keep pressing on. It's just like running a race. Once you start a race, there's no stopping and resting. If you want to win, you've got to run with your eyes fixed on the goal in front of you.

The cardinal sin of any track runner is to let his eyes waver from the finish line. Any good runner knows that he runs with his eyes fixed on *one* object alone — the finish line — and he never takes his eyes off of it. In the Christian race, the goal is the Lord Jesus Christ, and those of us who are running this race must never let our eyes waver either, if we're going to be successful.

I remember one race I lost because I did just that: I allowed my eyes to waver from the goal. I will never forget it. I was out on the track running with everything I had, but suddenly I realized that I couldn't see or hear any runners next to me. I had the sensation that I was running out there all alone! I began reasoning in my mind. I thought, *You were so intent on running that you didn't hear it, but a false start was called. Everyone else is back at the starting line, but you're running out here all by yourself, and you look like a real fool, boy!*

As this argument was going on in my mind, I stole a glance across the track. I was running on the outside lane, and when I looked across, I saw another runner in lane one. We were leading the race by about seven yards ahead of everyone else, and that's why I hadn't heard or seen the other runners beside me.

We were just coming up on the finish line when I had taken that one fateful glance across the track. That one glance cost me half a stride. Moments later we both hit the finish line, and when that tape hit — it hit my opponent high at his chest, and it hit me at my waist. I was one hundredth of a second behind him! That one momentary glance away from the finish line cost me the race, all because I took my eyes off the goal! I had been ahead of that other runner by one step, but when I allowed doubt to enter my mind and I believed a lie, I got my eyes off the goal!

That same thing can happen to you as you run this race for God! If you allow him to, the devil will begin to talk to your mind, and if you believe what he says and take your eyes off of God, you'll lose ground. If you allow the devil to whisper his thoughts of defeat and discouragement and doubt and unbelief in your ear, you won't be able to keep your eyes on the goal either.

Never allow the enemy's thoughts to captivate your thinking. Never entertain his thoughts in your mind or allow them to linger — thoughts such as, "You're never going to make it." "It's too late for you now." "You're no good." "God's promises are just not going to come true for *you.*" If you give in and allow those thoughts to linger in your mind, the enemy will keep you from receiving God's best for your life.

Keep your eye on the goal — Jesus! You'll lose the race if you get your eyes off the goal. Get your eyes off man. Get your eyes off your own shortcomings and mistakes! God never said you were going to run this race in your own strength, anyway! Quit relying on the arm of flesh — yours or anyone else's! I'll tell you a little secret: It's not the arm of flesh that's going to put you over in life and make you a winner — it's Jesus and His unchanging Word!

The Man at the Gate Beautiful

The man at the Gate called Beautiful knew better than to take his eyes off the goal. We don't know how long he had been sitting beside that gate hoping for someone to come along and meet his needs, but we do know that he needed a miracle from God. His feet and ankle bones needed to be restored. The Bible says he had never walked in his life; he had been lame from his mother's womb.

ACTS 3:1-10
1   Now Peter and John went up together into the temple at the hour of prayer, being the ninth hour.
2   And a certain man lame from his mother's womb was carried, whom they laid daily at the gate of the temple which is called Beautiful, to ask alms of them that entered into the temple;
3   Who seeing Peter and John about to go into the temple asked an alms.
4   And Peter, fastening his eyes upon him with John, said, Look on us.
5   And he gave heed unto them, expecting to receive

something of them.

6   Then Peter said, Silver and gold have I none; but such as I have give I thee: In the name of Jesus Christ of Nazareth rise up and walk.

7   And he took him by the right hand, and lifted him up: and immediately his feet and ankle bones received strength.

8   And he leaping up stood, and walked, and entered with them into the temple, walking, and leaping, and praising God.

9   And all the people saw him walking and praising God:

10   And they knew that it was he which sat for alms at the Beautiful gate of the temple: and they were filled with wonder and amazement at that which had happened unto him.

Maybe this man had sat at the Gate Beautiful begging for years. Perhaps for years he had just been hoping someone would come along and offer to take him home and take care of him. When Peter said, "Look on us," perhaps this man thought, *Here it is! Someone is finally going to provide for me for the rest of my life.*

But when Peter said, "Silver and gold have I none," that man could have just dismissed Peter and John from his mind, and thought, *If they don't have any money for me, they don't have anything I want.* After all, he needed money so he could eat! What else could Peter and John possibly have for a lame man? But he must have made a decision to keep his expectation alive and to focus his attention on the words of Peter and John, because we know that he did receive from God. And we know that his faith must have grabbed ahold of something Peter and John said to him, because he rose up healed.

We have no documentation of it in the Word, but we can imagine that when Peter reached down to grab that man by his hand — to that lame man Peter's face probably changed from one of hundreds in the multitude who passed by the Gate Beautiful day after day, into the face of someone who genuinely cared. We can imagine that in this lame man's perception even the very hands of Peter changed as they reached down to help him in his need. Those hands that had hauled in fishing nets as the hot sun beat down in that eastern sky; those hands that had cleaned fish and had been used to doing the roughest kind of work; suddenly those hands reached out to help this poor lame man in need. And in a certain sense, as part of the Body of Christ, Peter's hands did become the "hands" of Jesus Christ extended through this rough fisherman as they reached down to help a crippled man in need. Then Peter spoke those unforgettable words that changed a crippled man's life: "... *In the name of Jesus Christ of Nazareth rise up and walk"* (v. 6)!

The love of God through Peter reached out to this lame man and the man's ankle bones were strengthened and he was made whole. In a moment of time, the lame man knew he wouldn't have to spend the rest of his life begging, and he began to walk and leap and praise God!

The lame man kept his focus on what he was about to receive, and his hopes were not disappointed! After all, when Peter first approached him, he could have said, "Well, if you don't have any money, get out of here. You're blocking the way from someone who *will* give me some money!" But if he had taken his eyes off what God was about to do for him, he would have missed his blessing from God.

God will reach down and meet you right where you are too! Don't let your eyes waver from the goal! Do not let your eyes be fixed on the problem or the circumstance you are facing, because with God's help you can go around any obstacle and you can overcome any problem! I don't care what kind of condition you are in! I don't care what kind of desperate circumstance the enemy has tried to encompass round about you to wear you out! I don't care what the symptoms say! I don't care how many times your checkbook shows a zero balance, or who has told you that there is no use trying, you're just a failure in life!

You see, it doesn't make any difference what man *does;* it doesn't make any difference what man *says;* it doesn't make any difference what man *thinks.* I'm going to tell you what does make a difference though. It makes a difference what Jesus *said* in His Word. And Jesus said in His Word that if you knock, He *will* open. If you ask, He will answer. And Jesus said, "If you keep your eyes on the mark — the prize of the high calling — you will come behind in no good gift" (Phil. 3:14; 1 Cor. 1:7). God's Word works, no matter what the circumstances are! I know what the Word of God says! *"For with God nothing shall be impossible"* (Luke 1:37). It also says, "No Word from God shall return to Him void, without accomplishing what it was sent forth to do" (Isa. 55:11). If you will refuse to quit, and if you will put all your trust in God's Word, you can have whatever you need from God! Put pressure on God's Word, and watch the Word fight your battles for you.

Many of you have been believing God for something, and you've wondered how in the world it is ever going to come to pass. The thought has entered your mind, *I guess this isn't for me. There's no way I can achieve this so it must not be God.* But I'm going to tell you something: Those thoughts that you can't have what God has promised you are from the enemy! That's not God! God's Word says that Jesus Christ is the same yesterday, today, and forever (Heb. 13:8). The power of God is the same forever and your faith and trust in God will see you through to victory.

Jesus Is Our Example

Defeat isn't part of Jesus' nature. Jesus, the One who walked upon the face of this earth doing mighty exploits; Jesus, the One who died on the Cross; Jesus, the One who the Bible says became sin, who knew no sin, that we might become the righteousness of God in Christ. That same Jesus knows no defeat! That wonderful Savior does not know defeat so why should we, the Church, who are part of His Body accept defeat in our lives! The Bible also declares that Jesus took the keys of death and hell, and that He ascended on High where He ever lives to make intercession for you and me (Rev. 1:18; Heb 7:25). Therefore, we do not need to fail in anything we do!

REVELATION 1:18
18 I am he that liveth, and was dead; and, behold, I am alive for evermore, Amen; and have the keys of hell and of death.

HEBREWS 7:25
25 Wherefore he [Jesus] is able also to save them to the uttermost that come unto God by him, seeing he ever liveth to make intercession for them.

Because Jesus purchased our total redemption at the Cross of Calvary, there is no problem that is unsolvable, and there is no fear that is unconquerable, if we will believe

God and put our trust in His Word! Your needs may be pressing, but your uncompromised faith in God will see you through to victory! All the onslaughts of hell and all the forces of evil combined cannot vanquish the power of a steadfast, uncompromising faith in God. If you will refuse to compromise your faith, God will see to it that the power that has been invested in the Church of the Lord Jesus Christ will be effectual in your life because you have dared to believe Him!

1 THESSALONIANS 2:13
13 For this cause also thank we God without ceasing, because when ye received the word of God which ye heard of us, ye received it not as the word of men, but as it is in truth, the word of God, which EFFECTUALLY WORKETH ALSO IN YOU THAT BELIEVE.

I want you to know that there has never been a problem that has been placed into the hands of God that has received less than heaven's best. Stand your ground against the enemy! The enemy will always try to bluff you; He will always try to make you think that he can overcome you, but *the Word of God* says that Satan is a defeated foe. Speak the Word against the enemy, and put him on the run by using the Name of Jesus!

God doesn't hand out substitutes for His blessings. He doesn't hand out rhinestones for diamonds. His Word declares that when you ask for bread, He doesn't give you a stone; or if you ask for a fish, He doesn't give you a serpent (Matt. 7:9,10). He's never turned away one of His children who has come to Him in simple childlike faith. Not once has God ever said, "I'm sorry, heaven is out of that blessing; we don't have any more." Or, "I'm sorry, you'll have to settle for less than the best." Or, "I'm sorry, I can't do that for you because I don't know how"! Or have you ever heard God tell you when you approach His throne, "I don't have time for you today. Go away." No! God's ears are always open to hear the cry of the righteous (Ps. 34:15).

God gives the best heaven has to offer to those who have determined to commit their lives to Him and to walk in obedience to His will for their lives! God promises us in His Word that He will withhold no good thing from those who walk uprightly (Ps. 84:11).

Resolve today to renew your commitments to God, and to His will for your life. Put away from your mind the thoughts and feelings of failure and hopelessness. Go to God afresh in faith believing that if you ask anything according to His will, He hears you. And the Bible says that if you know He hears you, then you know that you have your petition (1 John 5:14,15). Determine today to take authority over the enemy in whatever area of your life he's tried to hold you in bondage. Then keep your eyes off of the circumstances, and keep them fixed on God and His Word. Dare to believe God, and you'll walk away in victory!